WORLD CUP LEGENDS

Once every four years, the greatest players and teams from around the globe come together in a celebration of the beautiful game. Packed with colour, excitement, passion and drama, the World Cup has the world glued to their televisions as the biggest names in football dazzle on the ultimate stage. From Pelé and Maradona to Ronaldo, Moore and Marta, some of the most iconic names in the history of football are synonymous with the World Cup.

In this book you'll find a host of fascinating features on the aforementioned stars, as well as the Magnificent Magyars of the 1950s and the best side never to win the World Cup – the Cruyff-inspired Dutch team of the 1970s. We also bring you the 50 greatest players to grace the tournament, take you on a journey back through some of the World Cup's most memorable moments, and meet the players who illuminated the 2023 Women's World Cup.

CONTENTS

6 — 50 GREATEST WORLD CUP PLAYERS
We look back at 50 of the best players to grace world football's biggest stage

22 — THE FIRST CHAMPIONS
Uruguay etch their name in history as the inaugural World Cup's winners

24 — PELÉ
The rags-to-riches tale of the World Cup's most iconic star

32 — TOP 10: SCORERS
We take a look at some of the World Cup's leading goalscorers

34 — LEGENDS OF THE '66 WORLD CUP
Relive England's famous victory as told by those who were there

40 — EUSÉBIO NETS FOUR
One of the all-time greats stakes his claim as a World Cup legend

42 — MARACANAZO
The story of Brazil's devastating defeat in the 1950 World Cup final

46 — TOP 10: GOALKEEPERS
Ten of the best goalkeepers to have graced the world stage

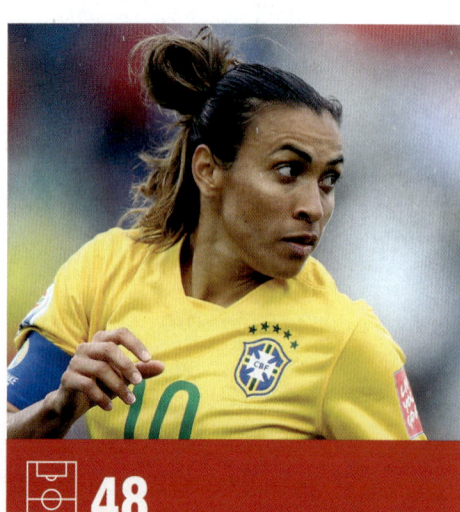

48 — MARTA
The rise of Brazil's silky superstar from playing without shoes to the global stage

52 — TWO ICONS SWAP SHIRTS
Brazil's Pelé and England's Bobby Moore swap shirts in a famous show of respect

54 — MARADONA
From the glory of 1986 to the shame of 1994, we explore the highs and lows of the Argentinian hero's World Cup career

64 — 10 LEGENDARY WORLD CUP COACHES
Meet some of the most iconic and groundbreaking managers to win football's ultimate prize

72 — ZIDANE
The story of the two World Cup finals that defined Zinedine Zidane's glittering international career

80 — TOTAL FOOTBALL AND THE BIRTH OF THE MODERN GAME
The story of the best side to never lift football's most prestigious prize

84 — TOP 10: WORLD CUP GOALS
A selection of the World Cup's most memorable strikes

86 — THE MAGNIFICENT MAGYARS
Charting the rise and fall of football's first revolutionary force

92 — BERGKAMP'S BRILLIANCE
The Dutch master scores one of the World Cup's greatest goals

"MARADONA WAS AT HIS PEAK FOR THE 1986 WORLD CUP IN MEXICO"

CONTENTS

"ZIDANE SAW RED AND PAVED THE WAY FOR ITALY"

94 RONALDO
After a nightmare in 1998, Ronaldo was Brazil's hero just four years later

100 TOP 10: WORLD CUP KITS
The World Cup's most vibrant, memorable and iconic kits

102 FRANZ BECKENBAUER
The footballer nicknamed 'Der Kaiser' led West Germany to glory in 1974 and then repeated the feat from the dugout in 1990

108 SPAIN'S TIKI-TAKA REVOLUTION
The story of Spain's 2010 World Cup winners and how they changed the way the game was played forever

112 KILLING THE DREAM
Germany send Brazil crashing out of their World Cup with a 7-1 thrashing that sent ripples across the globe

114 TOP 10: FUTURE LEGENDS
We try to predict which young stars could etch their names into the history books by starring on the biggest stage

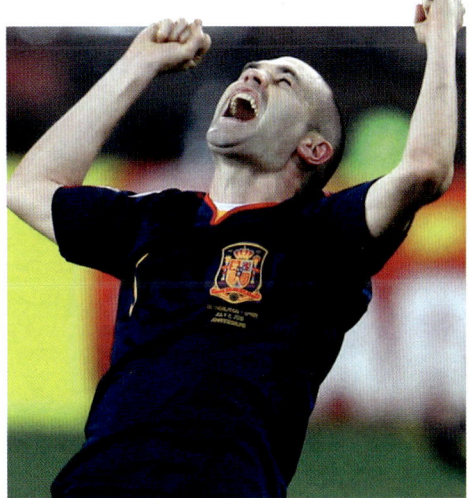

116 ENGLAND WIN A SHOOTOUT
How England exorcised the ghosts of the past to clinch a historic victory on a famous night in Moscow

118 TOP 10: WORLD CUP UPSETS
We look back at ten of the biggest World Cup shocks

120 MESSI WINS THE BIGGEST PRIZE
On a dramatic night in Qatar the game's greatest player finally got his hands on the one prize that had eluded him

122 11 STARS OF THE 2023 WOMEN'S WORLD CUP
Meet the players who illuminated the ninth edition of the greatest competition in the women's game

128 RUSSO FIRES THE LIONESSES INTO THE FINAL
Latching onto a sublime through ball, England's Alessia Russo smashes home her nation's third goal against Australia to book Sarina Wiegman's team a place in the World Cup final

WORLD CUP LEGENDS

50 GREATEST WORLD CUP PLAYERS

Hundreds of players have appeared at the World Cup since it began way back in 1930, but only a chosen few have dominated the competition and etched their names into history

One of the most exciting things about the World Cup is seeing some of the globe's very best footballers strut their stuff on the biggest stage of all. It's a joy to watch footballers in their prime perform to the best of their ability, and while the most skilful teams don't always win, talent generally finds a way to shine.

To that end, we have players with sublime skill, and others who are so solid in defence that almost nothing will get past them. If anything, it's a disappointment that we didn't get to see all of the greats; had George Best, Alfredo Di Stéfano, George Weah and Ryan Giggs played in the tournament, for instance, they would certainly have made the list.

But that's not to say our top 50 is in any way anaemic; chances are any one of these players would make it into any team the world has ever assembled, club or country. All have shown brilliance or made their mark on the World Cup in ways that will always stick in the mind, and as such, we present them here in no particular order.

50 GREATEST WORLD CUP PLAYERS

LIONEL MESSI

01 After tasting defeat in the 2014 World Cup final and crashing out in the Round of 16 in 2018, many feared that Messi would never win the ultimate prize. Then came the winter of 2022 and a World Cup in Qatar that saw Messi on a mission. After overcoming a shock opening defeat to Saudi Arabia, he fired Argentina to glory with seven goals and three assists to finally clinch the crown he'd always craved the most.

The modern game's greatest player is now a World Cup winner

CARLOS ALBERTO TORRES

02 Regarded as one of football's finest defenders, Carlos Alberto missed out in 1966 but captained Brazil in the final of the 1970 World Cup. A pass by Pelé in the 86th minute gifted him the golden opportunity to hammer home the fourth and final goal against Italy. It's still considered one of the best goals ever scored in the tournament.

ROBERTO CARLOS

03 A mainstay of the Brazilian team going into three World Cups, Carlos' skill at left-back helped his team reach the final in 1998. But while they lost against France 3-0, the number six emerged victorious four years later. All in all, he ended up playing an impressive 17 World Cup matches.

ROGER MILLA

04 Roger Milla retired from international football in 1987 having made his first World Cup appearance for Cameroon five years earlier. But he came out of retirement aged 38 in 1990, scoring four World Cup goals and enthralling fans with his corner flag dance. He played again in 1994, becoming the oldest goalscorer at 42 when he put one past Russia.

PAUL BREITNER

05 Breitner made 14 appearances for West Germany and scored four goals over two tournaments. None of these were more important than the 25th-minute penalty to equalise against the Netherlands in Munich in 1974, paving the way for eventual victory and West Germany's second World Cup. He also scored in the final of 1982, but on that occasion ended up on the losing side as Italy defeated West Germany 3-1.

WORLD CUP LEGENDS

LEV YASHIN

06 **It was no surprise to see Soviet Union goalkeeper Yashin appear on the official 2018 Russia World Cup poster.** His dominance between the sticks saw him shout instructions at his defence and collect crosses off the line in a manner that was unique at the time. He ended up playing 12 times in four World Cups, keeping four clean sheets.

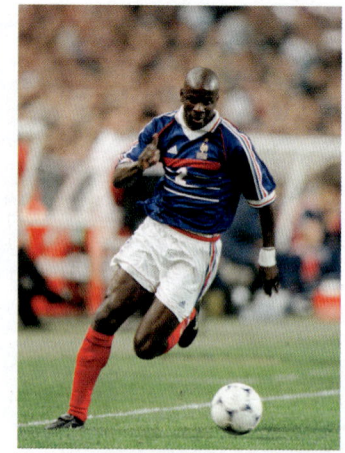

LILIAN THURAM

07 **The defender only scored twice for France, but what important goals they were.** Finding his team 1-0 down against Croatia in the 1998 semi-final, he equalised within a minute before bagging the winner in the 70th minute. He went on to become a world champion, adding a European Championship two years later.

KARL-HEINZ RUMMENIGGE

08 **Although Rummenigge lost two finals – in 1982 and 1986 – the winger was impressive in both tournaments.** He scored a hat-trick against Chile in the 1982 group stages and grabbed a goal in the 1986 final as West Germany attempted to get back into the game against Argentina. He scored nine World Cup goals in 19 appearances.

○ Rummenigge scored 45 goals in 95 appearances for West Germany

GIUSEPPE MEAZZA

09 **The Italian national team, blessed with prolific goalscorer Meazza's talents, won two consecutive World Cups.** Nicknamed 'Il Genio' ('The Genius'), he scored the only goal against Spain in the 1934 quarter-final en route to victory (subsequently being named the tournament's best player), and he captained Italy to a 4-2 win over Hungary in 1938.

50 GREATEST WORLD CUP PLAYERS

GORDON BANKS

10 As one of the best goalkeepers to grace a football field, Banks played in every game for England during the 1966 World Cup. Emerging victorious, he would prepare for games by chewing gum, spitting on his hands and smoothing them over. He could then lick his palms to make them sticky as opposition players headed his way.

OLIVER KAHN

11 Even though Kahn was named in the Germany World Cup squads in both 1994 and 1998, he only became the first-choice goalkeeper in 2002. For keeping five clean sheets and only letting in three goals (two in the final against Brazil) he was awarded the Golden Ball - the only goalkeeper ever to have achieved this feat to date.

MIA HAMM

12 Hailed as the first female football superstar, Mia Hamm spearheaded a formidable USA team that won it all. Having made her debut at just 15, Hamm went on to score 158 goals (a record when she retired in 2004) over 276 appearances that saw her win two of the four World Cups she competed in (the 1991 and 1999 editions respectively) as well as Olympic gold in 1996 and 2004.

Hamm scored in every World Cup she played in

WORLD CUP LEGENDS

GIANLUIGI BUFFON

13 With 176 caps, goalkeeper Buffon has not only played more games for Italy than any other footballer; he has appeared in five World Cup tournaments (1998, 2002, 2006, 2010 and 2014, playing in the latter four). His finest was the winning year of 2006, setting a record for conceding just two goals in seven matches with five clean sheets.

DANIEL PASSARELLA

14 Passarella is considered to be Argentina's greatest defender, but he could also score lots of goals. Calm and collected, he captained the 1978 winning team and, although he missed the tournament due to illness, he was named for 1986, making him the only Argentinian to be in both of the country's winning squads.

Baresi was one of the greatest defenders in world football

FRANCO BARESI

15 Defender Baresi won the 1982 tournament with Italy, and while he came third in 1990, he was named in the FIFA World Cup All-Star Team. He became captain in 1994, but despite missing a penalty in a final Brazil won, simply being there was surprising considering that he underwent surgery to his knee just three weeks before.

50 GREATEST WORLD CUP PLAYERS

Klose holds the record for the most goals scored at World Cup finals

MIROSLAV KLOSE

16 **When striker Klose retired from international football on 11 August 2014, he did so a very happy player.** After all, just months before, Germany had won the World Cup for the first time since 1990. Klose had also scored in the 7-1 drubbing of Brazil in the semi-final, which saw him become the World Cup's all-time top scorer with 16 goals, just edging Ronaldo. That was his record-breaking fourth World Cup semi, and the goal (in addition to the one he scored against Ghana) put clear daylight between him and Gerd Müller as Klose became Germany's top goalscorer.

FERENC PUSKÁS

17 **Hungary's influential captain Puskás was easily the best player in the 1954 World Cup.** He was also part of one of the greatest sides the tournament has ever seen. As a talented inside left, this stocky player would practise his ball skills by juggling with a tennis ball, and his amazing shooting prowess was on display in the very first game. He scored two of nine goals against South Korea and helped Hungary to the final, but despite Puskás opening the scoring, they were beaten 3-2 by West Germany. Still, the man they called the Galloping Major due to his role in Hungary's army epitomised the 'Mighty Magyars', and his thunderous left foot will never be forgotten.

Zidane was France's hero in the 1998 final but was dramatically sent off in the 2006 final against Italy

ZINEDINE ZIDANE

18 **Zidane won the World Cup with France in 1998, and he was certainly no bit-part player.** He scored twice in the 3-0 final defeat of Brazil in front of a home crowd at the Parc des Princes in Paris, and while they were his only goals, it added the World Cup to one of the most enviable honours lists in football. What set him apart was his composure with the ball and his knack of being able to pierce defences at the right moment. His passing was impeccable and his dribbling crisp. The World Cup victory saw his face projected on the Arc de Triomphe.

HOMARE SAWA

19 **Having exploded onto the international scene at 15 years of age with four goals on her debut, Homare Sawa enjoyed a glittering 22-year career with the Japanese national team.** Competing in an incredible six World Cup finals (1995, 1999, 2003, 2007, 2011 and 2015), the diminutive midfielder enjoyed her crowning moment during the 2011 tournament in Germany. Scoring four goals en route to the final, she netted a crucial extra-time equaliser to draw Japan level at 2-2 with the USA in the final (one of 83 goals scored in 205 appearances) before watching her teammates complete the comeback with a 3-1 victory on penalties. Sawa won the Golden Ball and Boot awards to round off a stunning personal campaign.

FRANZ BECKENBAUER

20 **Pelé was full of praise for Beckenbauer, famed for his stylish defending and ability as captain of West Germany.** He influenced the nation both on and off the pitch as his country secured the World Cup in 1974. He then went on to win the World Cup in 1990 as Germany's manager.

GARY LINEKER

21 **Lineker knew how to find the net.** As England's most successful World Cup striker with ten goals to his name, his clinical approach to the game saw him shoot six past opponents in the 1986 tournament (winning him the Golden Boot) and grab a further four in 1990. Three of those goals came in a blistering first-half hat-trick against Poland in the final group game of 1986, and it only cemented the reputation of a player known not only as 'Mister Nice Guy' but as a footballer with pace and an uncanny ability to find space in front of goal.

○ Zoff made his Italy debut in 1968 and went on to win 112 caps for his country

DINO ZOFF

22 **Zoff was aged 40 and 133 days when he lifted the World Cup trophy for Italy on 11 July 1982 against West Germany – the oldest player to win the tournament.** As Italy's first-choice goalkeeper and captain during that summer, he kept two clean sheets and made a jaw-dropping reaction save in the second round against Brazil, ensuring his team preserved their 3-2 lead and progressed. Zoff was named in the All-Star team, and he was heralded as 1982's best goalkeeper. He also appeared in the previous three World Cups, keeping three clean sheets in 1978 as Italy came fourth.

50 GREATEST WORLD CUP PLAYERS

RONALDINHO

23 **Starring alongside Ronaldo and Rivaldo, Ronaldinho was part of a fearsome trinity that seemed almost destined to win Brazil the World Cup in 2002.** His curling free kick from 40 yards in the quarter-final saw England's David Seaman floundering as the ball floated into the top-left corner of the goal. But he will also be remembered for the joy he seemed to get from football and the freedom he appeared to have with the ball at his feet. Able to instantly change pace and pass without a glance, he back-passed and step-overed his way to glory.

ROBERTO BAGGIO

24 **In the USA in 1994, Baggio had the tournament of his life, and it earned him the Silver Ball as the second-best player.** The forward was undoubtedly Italy's top dog, scoring five goals and helping his country reach the final. This, however, is when Baggio's shine dimmed. After a 0-0 draw with Brazil after extra time, the game went to penalties. Baggio needed to score to keep Italy in with a chance, but he put the decisive kick high over the bar and into the crowd, leaving him distraught and Brazil champions. Even so, he also scored in the 1990 and 1998 tournaments, making him the only Italian to bag goals in three World Cup tournaments.

FABIO CANNAVARO

○ Cannavaro was one of a long line of world-class Italian defenders

25 **As captain, acclaimed defender Cannavaro led Italy to victory in the 2006 World Cup final, impressing fans by marshalling an almost impenetrable back line (Italy conceded just two goals during the tournament).** His strength, positional sense, awareness and timing earned him the nickname 'Il Muro di Berlino' ('the Berlin Wall'), and this highly athletic player, who was as good in the air as he was on the ground, even went on to become the FIFA World Player of the Year; the first defender to win the award since it began in 1991. All in all, this tenacious player made 18 appearances over four World Cups.

13

WORLD CUP LEGENDS

RIVALDO

26 **Think of Rivaldo, and you immediately conjure up images of his bending free kicks, tricky feints and intricate dribbling.** You may also think about that match against Turkey in 2002 when the ball hit his arm and he fell to the floor clutching his face - earning opponent Hakan Ünsal a red card. Cheating aside, there is no doubting Rivaldo's skill, and it ultimately helped earn him and his Brazil team a World Cup victory that year.

MARIO ZAGALLO

27 **Winning the World Cup twice as a player (in 1958 and 1962) is always a triumph, but doing so twice as a manager and assistant manager is something else.** To that end, left-winger Zagallo is about as ingrained in Brazil's success over the years as anyone could be, and he deserves the accolades he receives, even though some said he was fortunate to be playing. On the pitch, he was well-known for his runs from deep and his versatility. He also displayed tenacity and a never-say-die spirit. Favouring tireless hard work as well as style, he scored in Brazil's famous 5-2 defeat of Sweden in 1958.

JOHAN NEESKENS

28 **The Dutchman was a fantastic tackler and a dead ball specialist.** He took part in two World Cup campaigns, with the Netherlands cruelly losing out in the finals of both 1974 and 1978.

Hurst made his name with a hat-trick in the 1966 World Cup final against West Germany

GEOFF HURST

29 **Hurst had only debuted for England against West Germany on 23 February 1966 - just months before the World Cup began - and he only gained a place in England's starting World Cup line-up in the quarter-final against Argentina after Jimmy Greaves became injured.** He scored in that game and went on to assist Bobby Charlton in the semis, impressing manager Alf Ramsey so much that he was given a place in the final. Hurst repaid the faith by cancelling out Helmut Haller's opening goal, but the game ultimately went into extra time. Hurst struck twice more to win the day, securing the only World Cup final hat-trick to date.

MARIO KEMPES

30 **Argentina's explosive attacker scored two against the Netherlands in the 1978 World Cup final, which not only eased them to victory but saw him end the tournament as both the top goalscorer (with six) and the best player.** Those who watched him play would agree that his shot was devastating, and his calmness under pressure was impressive. Yet he was also far from unassuming, playing with panache and becoming instantly noticeable for his personal style as well as his close ball control. For Argentinians he was a national hero, although the country crashed out in the second round of 1982 - a tournament that saw the introduction of a certain Diego Maradona.

ZICO

31 Referred to as the 'white Pelé', Zico was a creative attacking midfielder whose eye for goal and technical skill were put to particularly good use in 1982. His goals helped Brazil win against Scotland, New Zealand and Argentina, so it was a shame for him that his country did not progress further than the second round.

In some ways it was a disappointment perhaps only matched by his goal in the opening match of the 1978 World Cup being ruled out. Still, such was his worth, Brazil worked hard to get him fit after a serious knee injury in 1986. In that tournament, he came on as a second-half substitute in the quarter-final against France. Unfortunately, he missed a penalty and Brazil crashed out to France. There was no faulting his prodigious work ethic, however.

○ Still just 24, Mbappé has scored 12 goals across two World Cups

KYLIAN MBAPPÉ

32 If the question of which player would take up the mantle from Messi and Ronaldo to become the game's new great wasn't answered in 2018, it certainly was in 2022. Kylian Mbappé is without doubt the most naturally gifted and devastatingly explosive talent to burst onto the world stage since the emergence of the legends he looks set to emulate. Blessed with blistering pace and a deadly eye for goal, at just 18 he was integral to France winning the 2018 World Cup and reaching the final four years later in Qatar. After pillaging three goals in the group stages and two in the Round of 16, Mbappé failed to find the net against England or Morocco as Les Bleus set up a mouthwatering clash against Messi's Argentina in the final. It was therefore only right to remind the world of his immense talent by becoming only the second player in history to score a World Cup final hat-trick. He may have lost in Lusail, but with at least two World Cups left in him, few would bet against Mbappé leading France to glory again.

GERD MÜLLER

33 Nicknamed 'Bomber der Nation' – or 'the Nation's Bomber' – West German striker Müller scored 14 goals in the two World Cups in which he appeared (1970 and 1974). He quickly became an icon for winning the 1974 World Cup with a decisive goal in the 43rd minute against the Netherlands. Just as memorable was his winning goal in the quarter-final of 1970 against then-world champions England, who were 2-0 up after 49 minutes. West Germany fought back to draw level before Müller struck the winner in extra time.

He would startle opponents with a rapid burst of pace over a short distance and could throw his short body into the air above taller players to win countless aerial duels. Many an opposing footballer could only watch as he turned tightly with great balance, yet he was also humble and reserved even in victory.

WORLD CUP LEGENDS

CAFU

34 His country's most capped footballer with 142 appearances, and it's easy to see why. An amazing full-back, Cafu could burst down the right side of the pitch, essentially becoming an attacking right winger. When Jorginho was injured in the 1994 final, manager Carlos Alberto Parreira had no worries putting Cafu in to replace him, even though he'd only made two appearances as a sub prior.

By the time 1998 rolled around, Cafu was a firmly established international. Brazil were beaten in the final, but they had better luck in 2002 when, as captain, Cafu led them to a 2-0 victory over Germany. During that tournament he was relentless, flying past opponents en route to the trophy.

GARRINCHA

35 Manuel Francisco dos Santos, to give his full name, won the World Cup twice – in 1958 and 1962 – but it was the latter tournament that made his name.

He stepped in for the injured Pelé and rose to the occasion, so much so that he was named the best player in 1962 and became joint top goalscorer.

Garrincha's strength was his remarkable control of the ball, amazing dribbling and powerful shooting. He was especially good with free kicks and corners, and he'd relish toying with opponents, not being afraid to show them up by displaying his talent to the max.

○ Gazza bursts into tears as England are beaten by West Germany in the 1990 semi-final

PAUL GASCOIGNE

36 Most remember Gascoigne – or Gazza – for the semi-final in 1990 when he earned himself a yellow card for a foul on West Germany's Thomas Berthold and promptly broke down in tears knowing that he'd be unable to play in the final. In the event, England didn't make it that far, but the memory sticks, as does the feeling that such a great talent should have graced more than six games at a solitary World Cup.

Why? Simply because Gazza was one of England's great talents. A flawed creative genius, he played as an attacking midfielder and his passing accuracy was superb, as was his protective skills on the ball, not to mention his great pace and strength. It's really unfortunate that his off-field activities clouded a great talent, but for many England fans he helped define 1990. If it wasn't for his assist to Mark Wright to get the winner against Egypt, England may never have got out of the group stage.

50 GREATEST WORLD CUP PLAYERS

PAOLO ROSSI

37 **Rossi's preparation for the 1982 World Cup had been far from ideal.** He had just returned from a two-year ban for his involvement in the 1980 betting scandal, 'Totonero', which found many Italian football players guilty of match-fixing, and he had only played three times before the World Cup kicked off.

Manager Enzo Bearzot wanted him, however, and so the number 20 started in the opening stalemate against Poland. He came into his own during the second stage, scoring a hat-trick against Brazil. He then got two against Poland in the semis and opened the scoring in the final as Italy beat West Germany 3-1.

All was forgiven (although Rossi always denied being involved in match-fixing), Bearzot's decision to choose and then stick with him having paid off handsomely. But then Rossi was always intelligent, agile and prolific, and what he lacked in strength he made up for with incisive finishing and positional sense. His six goals in 1982 earned him the Golden Boot.

MICHEL PLATINI

38 **The French side of the 1980s was exceptional, and this was in great part down to the attacking midfielder Platini.** The team had learned their lessons from 1978 when they were knocked out at the group stage. Although they only scraped through the groups in 1982, Platini got on the scoresheet against Kuwait and scored again against West Germany in the semis, eventually losing on penalties.

Platini was known to be one of the finest passers of the ball. He was also a prolific goalscorer, and he went on to lead France through the 1986 groups before scoring against Italy in the Round of 16 and Brazil in the quarters, a game they won on penalties.

Charlton was a key part of Alf Ramsey's World Cup-winning team in 1966

BOBBY CHARLTON

39 With his trademark combover blowing in the wind and his name famous the world over, the Busby Babe who survived the Munich air crash in 1958 and established himself in Matt Busby's Manchester United squad was a key player for England during the three tournaments in which he was selected (he didn't kick a ball in 1958 but starred in 1962, 1966 and 1970).

Renowned for his thunderous shooting, which he could perform with either foot, his simple yet confident dribbling and elegant style of play endeared him to both United and England supporters. Arguably the most gifted English football player in the national team, he carried himself with a sense of gentlemanliness, and he was absolutely crucial to England's World Cup triumph on home soil in 1966, opening the scoring in a 2-0 group-stage win over Mexico and netting both goals in a tense 2-1 semi-final defeat of Portugal.

WORLD CUP LEGENDS

○ Eusébio scored against Bulgaria, Brazil (2), North Korea (4), England and the Soviet Union during the 1966 World Cup

EUSÉBIO

40 England may have won the World Cup in 1966, but Eusébio won hearts across the world. Playing for Portugal, he was awarded the Golden Boot for his nine goals while showcasing superb dribbling skills, athleticism and speed.

Famed for his right foot and nicknamed 'the Black Panther', 1966 turned out to be Eusébio's only World Cup, and he certainly made the most of it. When Portugal fell behind by three goals against North Korea, he fought hard to score in the 27th, 43rd, 56th and 59th minutes, putting his country ahead before José Augusto de Almeida grabbed the fifth.

There was an uneasy feeling that he would do the same to England in the semi-final when he got a penalty in the 82nd minute. Yet while he buried the spot kick he couldn't spart another revival. Although they were knocked out by England, Portugal would go on to achieve their best-ever placing, beating the Soviet Union 2-1 (aided by a Eusébio goal) to finish third.

CHRISTINE SINCLAIR

41 Born in British Columbia in 1983, Christine Sinclair seemed destined for a career in football from the very start. With her father and an uncle having both played professionally, Sinclair began kicking a ball at four, and just 12 years later she made her debut for Canada.

An unerringly accurate striker, Sinclair is known for her diligent work rate and ability to bring teammates into play. Blessed with a vision that enables her to see opportunities before they appear, Sinclair has to date featured in five World Cups, scoring ten goals in 21 games to contribute to an incredible international total of 190 goals in 315 matches, a record that has seen her nominated for the World Player of the Year award eight times.

JAIRZINHO

42 So many Brazilian players from 1970 deserve to be named footballing icons, but none of them scored in every match that summer – except for Jairzinho, that is. He scored against Czechoslovakia, England and Romania in the group stages, grabbed the final goal against Peru in the quarters, helped Brazil to a 3-1 win in the semis, and popped up in the 71st minute of the final against Italy. He could have had two against England, if not for a crucial interception by Bobby Moore.

Jairzinho's performances earned the forward the nickname 'The Hurricane', and crowds rarely failed to gasp when he got up speed and pumped a lethal shot into the net. What's more, his success came despite him breaking his right leg twice.

XAVI

43 **In more recent times, few players have stood out as much as Xavi.** The midfielder appeared on the World Cup stage as a substitute against Paraguay in 2002, but his opportunities were limited. Not so in 2006 where he was soon showing how well he could find space and accurately pass to his teammates.

He reached football's summit at the 2010 World Cup. Stung by a shock 1-0 opening-day defeat to Switzerland, Spain rallied, with Xavi playing an integral role, enjoying a 91-per-cent passing success rate. He was named man of the match in the semi-final, and he worked incredibly well with Andrés Iniesta throughout the tournament, eventually getting himself listed in the World Cup All-Star Team. Spain lifted the trophy that summer but failed to get out of the group stage four years later, which only went to show just how integral the pass master had been for La Roja.

Xavi was instrumental to the Spanish team that won the World Cup in 2010

ROMÁRIO

44 **Romário's first World Cup in 1990 was a bit of disappointment, but then he had just recovered from a broken leg and he wasn't fully fit.** He only played for 65 minutes during that tournament before coming off for Müller in the match against Scotland. Far more impressive was 1994, however, when Romário made the World Cup his own.

A falling out with coach Carlos Alberto Parreira almost meant Romário didn't go to the USA that year. Only a furore back home saw him recalled to help get Brazil through a knife-edge qualifier. It was a wise decision, and one Parreira would never regret. Romário was irresistable at USA '94, scoring five goals to help fire Brazil to a fourth World Cup, displaying impressive ball control and an effectiveness at cutting past defenders. His skills rightfully earned him the Golden Ball for being the best player of the tournament.

WORLD CUP LEGENDS

JUST FONTAINE

45 Fontaine set a high standard when he lit up the World Cup of 1958, scoring a mammoth 13 goals – a record that stands to this day. Making it even more remarkable is the fact it was achieved over six matches, so he was off to a flying start before the group stage was out.

He continued his streak into the quarter-finals with two goals against Northern Ireland. But although he scored against France in the semis, they were knocked out by Brazil, so Fontaine's efforts only saw his team earn third place. As a striker, however, he had few equals, which makes it all the more sad that he never played in another World Cup, injury forcing him to retire in 1962.

PELÉ

46 Edson Arantes do Nascimento is, to many minds, the greatest footballer to grace the World Cup. Playing in four tournaments, he made his debut in 1958 aged 17, and he competed in 1962, 1966 and, most notably, in 1970.

A prolific goalscorer, he had lightning pace and immense poise. He played with grace and could accurately shoot with great power with both feet. Unlike some talents, he worked with his teammates rather than as an individual. He was stylish and efficient: goalkeepers had little chance when he rolled up to take a penalty.

It is no surprise, then, that he holds the record for the most World Cup wins. His first tournament saw him score one against Wales in the quarter finals, three versus France in the semis and two in the final against Sweden. While he was injured for most of 1962 and persistently fouled through 1966, he accepted a call-up in 1970, playing six games and scoring six goals. Pelé really was the complete player.

○ Maradona's goal against England in 1986 is one of the best in World Cup history

DIEGO MARADONA

47 Ask any England fan to name a famous moment in World Cup football, and a good number will point to the quarter-final against Argentina in 1986. Having already displayed his brilliance, Maradona found himself heading towards goal, slipping past England's Glenn Hoddle with ease. His pass hit the foot of England's Steve Hodge, sending it towards the penalty area, at which point Maradona pounced – and hit it with his outside left hand. It thereafter became known as the 'Hand of God', but Argentina's captain Maradona was more than just that moment.

When Maradona had the ball, crowds would lick their lips with anticipation. With his physical strength and jaw-dropping dribbling skills, he was able to score five goals in 1986 and make five further assists. In doing so, he helped Argentina win the tournament that year before putting in another glorious set of displays four years later when he was named Italia '90's third-best player. While he marred his reputation by being sent home in 1994 for testing positive for ephedrine, there was a sense that his job was done, and his legendary status secured, making his nickname 'El Pibe de Oro' ('The Golden Boy') very apt. There will never be another like him.

50 GREATEST WORLD CUP PLAYERS

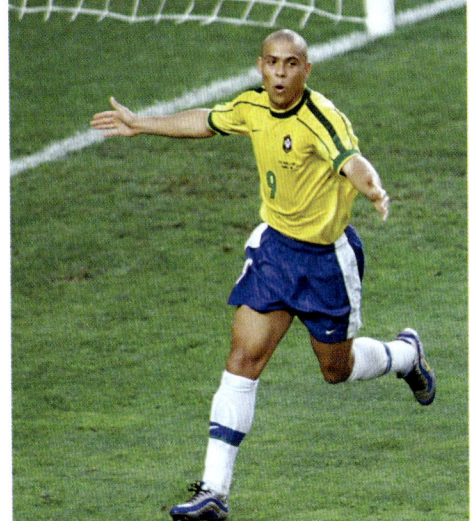

RONALDO

48 **With 15 goals over 19 matches, Ronaldo was, until 2014, the World Cup's top goalscorer.** But while he has since been pipped by Miroslav Klose, he will always be one of the greatest icons of the tournament.

He first appeared in 1998, when he scored four and was named the best player as Brazil were pipped by France. It set Brazil up nicely for 2002, however, when they won courtesy of two Ronaldo goals against Germany.

Yet that doesn't actually tell the full story. Prior to the 2002 finals, he had been out of the game for 15 months after rupturing the cruciate ligament in his right knee. That caused him to miss every Brazilian qualifier, so to come back in the tournament and perform so well was remarkable.

In his prime, he was one of the deadliest strikers football has ever seen.

JOHAN CRUYFF

49 **The Netherlands did not win the World Cup in 1974, yet pundits will tell you that the Dutch team was the more skilful and entertaining, and one of the main reasons for that was Johan Cruyff.**

If you could pinpoint a highlight, it would perhaps be the famous Cruyff turn of 1974, when he looked to be kicking the ball forward but instead scooped it backwards. It allowed him to turn tightly on the spot and head off in the opposite direction, leaving Sweden's Jan Olsen dumbfounded.

Such magic was also evident in the final, such as when, in the second minute, he orchestrated a move that ultimately led to the Netherlands winning a penalty and taking the lead against West Germany. It was just a shame he retired from international football in 1977, fearing kidnap in Argentina.

BOBBY MOORE

50 Even if West Ham's centre-half had not captained England to glory in 1966, he would still have proved his worth with a stunning display in that tournament, as well as those that preceded and followed in 1962 and 1970. But it will be 1966 that he will always be remembered for.

He didn't score (he only ever got two goals for England and they were both in friendlies) but it was his floating cross that helped Geoff Hurst get the opener in the final and his pinpoint pass that secured the infamous final Hurst goal that signalled it was all over.

What Moore lacked in pace and aerial ability he made up for with his football brain, and he is still widely regarded as the best defender of all time. Alf Ramsey didn't hesitate in making him captain even though he was aged just 22 years and 47 days. Moore repaid that faith in spades while becoming known as a gentleman of the game.

Skilled at free-kicks and frequently creating chances for Hurst, he was at his best on the big occasion, and people were so confident in his talent that Ron Greenwood, manager of West Ham, believed in 1965 that Moore would be the reason for an England victory since he had planned so well for the tournament.

○ England captain Bobby Moore lifts the World Cup in 1966

WORLD CUP LEGENDS

THE FIRST CHAMPIONS

30 JULY 1930
THE FIRST CHAMPIONS

Uruguay etch their name in history as the inaugural World Cup's winners

Every story has a beginning, and the story of the world's greatest sporting spectacle begins in 1930. That is the year in which the first World Cup was held in Uruguay, chosen as the hosts to coincide with the nation's celebration of the centenary of its first constitution.

The final was contested by Uruguay and Argentina in the Estadio Centenario, constructed especially for the tournament.

Uruguay struck first, scoring in the 12th minute, but Argentina fought back and went into the break leading 2-1.

In the second half, Uruguay took control again, scoring three goals and running out 4-2 winners. They became the first team to lift the famous Jules Rimet trophy, and etched their name in football history. The next day was declared a national holiday to celebrate the success.

Uruguay's glorious moment is not only significant for its people, but for football fans across generations. The success of that first tournament ensured the World Cup continued, treating us to all the exciting moments, awe-inspiring players, shock defeats and wonderful goals we've witnessed over the years. Without the success of the first tournament, the World Cup wouldn't be what it is today.

WORLD CUP LEGENDS

PELÉ

PELÉ: THE GREATEST

The rags-to-riches tale of the World Cup's most iconic star

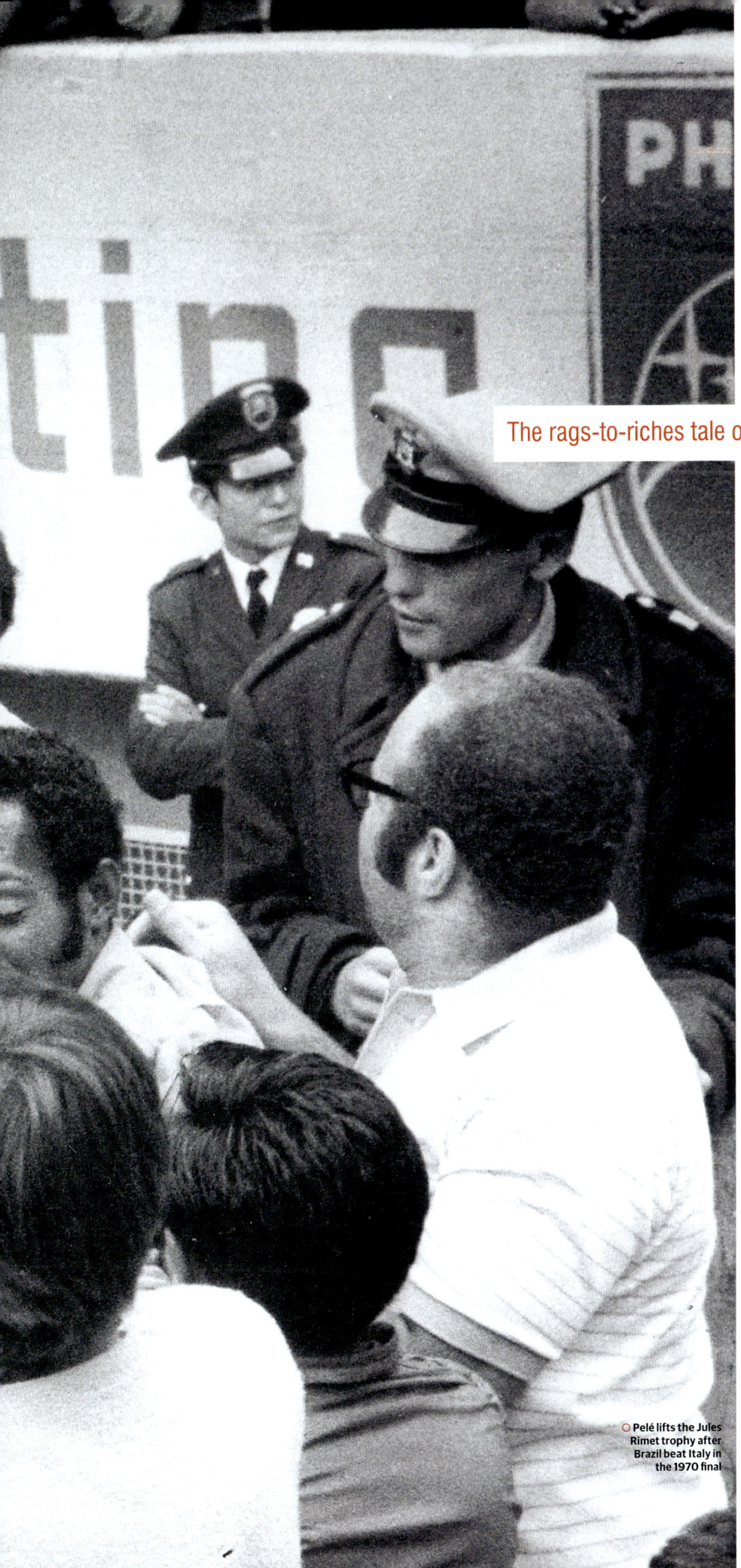

○ Pelé lifts the Jules Rimet trophy after Brazil beat Italy in the 1970 final

Stardom can flash like a supernova, fading into the darkness of obscurity as quickly as it erupts. Only the greatest of stars to have graced football's grandest stage shine with the enduring brightness that assures their status as legends. In that elite group, there is one that burns brighter than any other: the North Star of the World Cup, Pelé.

Pelé's legend is a testament both to his own incredible talent and the power of the World Cup. He played most of his club football for Santos in his native Brazil. In an age where it wasn't possible for fans to watch live football from all over the world and find clips of the next young talent on YouTube, it may as well have been on Mars as far as most of the world was concerned. It was the World Cup that gave Pelé the platform on which to showcase his ability to a global audience – his blend of athleticism and technique, artistry and end product, intelligence, desire and supreme dribbling skill. That is why his story is so intimately intertwined with the history of the tournament. The World Cup trophy is the treasure he claimed to complete his archetypal rise from rags to riches: the tale of an impoverished young kid who became a national hero and sporting icon through his exploits. It is the tournament that made him – and with his supreme talent, he helped make the tournament.

Pelé made his World Cup debut in Sweden in 1958. At only 17 years old, he was the youngest player ever to play in the tournament. He was already a star in his native Brazil, having finished the 1957 season as the league's top scorer at only 16 years of age while playing for Santos, but now he had the chance to do something even more special.

Pelé, like the rest of his countrymen, had not forgotten the national trauma known as 'the Maracanazo', or 'Maracanã Blow'. The name refers to Brazil's shock defeat to Uruguay in the final game of the 1950 World Cup, held on its own soil in a Maracanã Stadium packed with

25

WORLD CUP LEGENDS

PRAISE FROM PEERS

Johan Cruyff, Barcelona and Holland star:

"PELÉ WAS THE ONLY FOOTBALLER WHO SURPASSED THE BOUNDARIES OF LOGIC"

Just Fontaine, French striker and top scorer in the 1958 World Cup:

"WHEN I SAW PELÉ PLAY, IT MADE ME FEEL I SHOULD HANG UP MY BOOTS"

Ferenc Puskás, Real Madrid and Hungary legend:
"THE GREATEST PLAYER IN HISTORY WAS DI STEFANO. I REFUSE TO CLASSIFY PELÉ AS A PLAYER. HE WAS ABOVE THAT"

Bobby Moore, 1966 World Cup-winning England captain:

"PELÉ WAS THE MOST COMPLETE PLAYER I'VE EVER SEEN, HE HAD EVERYTHING"

Michel Platini, France legend and Ballon d'Or winner:

"THERE'S PELÉ THE MAN, AND THEN PELÉ THE PLAYER. AND TO PLAY LIKE PELÉ IS TO PLAY LIKE GOD"

200,000 people. Pelé screamed at a picture of Jesus in his father's room after the fateful final, asking why Brazil was being punished and telling the image of Christ that if he had been there, Brazil would have won. In Sweden, he had the chance to make good on this pledge.

Pelé arrived at the tournament with a knee injury, and didn't play in Brazil's first two games, a 3-0 victory over Austria and a 0-0 draw with England. He made his debut in his team's third group game against the USSR, impressing in a performance that included an assist for Vavá in a 2-0 win. Brazil moved on to the knockout stage, and it was here that the young Pelé began writing his legend in the lines drawn with his brilliant feet.

Midway through the second half in their quarter-final against Wales, and Pelé, standing on the penalty spot, received a headed ball on his chest with his back to goal. With a deft flick and turn, he left his marker floundering and poked the ball into the net. It was the only goal of the game, taking the team into a semi-final clash with France.

The France team of 1958 had some prolific talents of its own in the legendary Just Fontaine and Roger Piantoni. Indeed, both bagged a goal apiece - Fontaine in the first half and Piantoni in the second. This wasn't enough, however, to prevent the French from being swept away by an electric Brazil that netted five goals. Pelé led the charge, scoring in the 52nd, 64th and 75th minutes to become the youngest ever player to get a hat-trick in World Cup history.

In the final, Brazil came up against Sweden. That Brazil would win was far from a foregone conclusion: not only were Sweden the host nation, but no World Cup up to that point had been won by a nation outside its own continent. Sweden took the lead in the fourth minute through Nils Liedholm, but Brazil responded quickly, Vavá netting an equaliser - then another - to take Brazil into the break leading 2-1. In the 55th minute, Pelé broke yet another record, becoming the youngest scorer in a World Cup final as he netted one of the tournament's greatest ever goals. Waiting in the box, Pelé held off his marker as he jumped to meet a cross, twisting in the air to direct the ball towards the penalty spot with his chest. Another defender came out to close him down, but Pelé lifted the ball over his head, watched the ball drop from the sky and volleyed it powerfully into the bottom corner. Mário Zagallo followed up on Pelé's wonder goal to earn Brazil a 4-1 lead, before Simonsson pulled one back to give the hosts a slither of hope. It wasn't to be, however, as Pelé sealed the victory in stoppage time with a looping header that left the onrushing keeper stranded. The whistle blew, and he

PELÉ

○ Opposition players at the 1966 World Cup in England decided that the best way to stop Pelé was to kick him

broke down in tears of joy. The pain of the Maracanazo had been dulled, if not entirely healed. Brazil lifted its first World Cup trophy.

The 1958 World Cup triumph was a defining moment for both Pelé and Brazil. This victory helped establish Brazil as a global footballing superpower, and vindicated the nation's belief in a stylish brand of football that it wanted the world to admire. Indeed, the popular picture that now exists of what this great footballing nation represents - beautiful football, swashbuckling attacking, inspirational individual talent and international glory - started here. Pelé, at only 17, played an important part in that, making himself a star in the process. It was mind-boggling to see such a complete player at such a young age. He possessed pace, power, precise passing, vision, flair, a high work rate, anticipation, and an ability to finish. He had the whole world at his feet.

Yet Pelé's international career was not to continue in storybook fashion. When the 1962 World Cup in Chile rolled around, Brazil's star seemed primed to lead the team on to more glory. He started in apt fashion, creating one and scoring another after a mazy run where he beat four players in a 2-0 win over Mexico. In the next game against Czechoslovakia, however, Pelé was injured, keeping him out of the rest of the tournament. Fortunately,

○ Pelé was injured in Brazil's second game of the 1962 World Cup and wouldn't feature again in the tournament

WORLD CUP LEGENDS

○ Pelé (top) celebrates with his teammates during Brazil's 4-1 win over Italy in the 1970 World Cup final

PELÉ FACTS & FIGURES

MOST SUCCESSFUL LEAGUE GOALSCORER WITH 1281 GOALS IN 1363 GAMES

YOUNGEST WORLD CUP WINNER

ONLY PLAYER TO WIN 3 WORLD CUPS

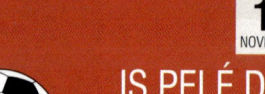
19 NOVEMBER IS PELÉ DAY AT SANTOS – AFTER THE DATE PELÉ SCORED HIS **1000TH GOAL**

SCORED HIS FIRST PROFESSIONAL GOAL ON HIS LEAGUE DEBUT AT 15 YEARS OLD

JOINT FIFA PLAYER OF THE CENTURY WITH DIEGO MARADONA

Pelé and Gerson both scored in the 1970 final, with Brazil becoming the first team to win the World Cup three times

that Brazil side was hardly starved for talent, and Pelé's teammates took up the slack, in particular a fellow footballing genius by the name of Garrincha. Brazil went on to triumph without Pelé, defeating Czechoslovakia 3-1 in the final.

Pelé's reputation was not diminished despite his absence for much of the 1962 tournament, and he was still the world's most famous talent when he came to England to play in the 1966 World Cup. But again, Pelé suffered from injury problems in a tournament where opposition players had evidently decided to kick him out of the game. He scored one goal in the opening match, missed the second through injury, and returned in the final game of the group stages, where he ended up limping around the pitch as he watched his team fall 3-1 to Portugal.

The 1966 failure left a bitter taste in the mouths of Brazil fans and Pelé himself. He vowed he would never play for Brazil in a World Cup again, frustrated by the deliberate fouling he had been subject to and the injuries he'd suffered as a result. Eventually, however, Pelé was persuaded to return to play in the 1970 World Cup in Mexico. We're grateful he did, because the team that he became part of was to go down in history as perhaps the greatest World Cup side of all time.

"BRAZIL'S SUPREME ATTACKING TALENT CAME UP AGAINST A MAGNIFICENT DEFENCE, PELÉ AGAINST BOBBY MOORE"

The side that went to Mexico in 1970 was phenomenally talented. The standout player in defence was the great Carlos Alberto, fittingly for a Brazil team, because of his rampaging attacking talent. In central midfield, the cultured Gerson was there to pull the strings alongside the tireless Clodoaldo. On the left was the graceful Rivelino, credited with innovating the flip flap, and on the opposite flank another of Brazil's many all-time greats, the dynamic Jairzinho. He complemented Rivelino's tendency to sit deep with a direct, pacey approach and eye for goal. Partnering Pelé was Tostão, a player with skill, vision, and most importantly for his partnership with Pelé, the intelligence to interchange with his star teammate, dropping deep when necessary and pushing forwards to make space in the hole for Pelé when appropriate.

This gifted team went one down to Czechoslovakia in the 11th minute of their first game of the group stages. A Rivelino goal brought them in level at the break, and Brazil exploded in the second half to swat their opponents out of their way. Pelé struck first to give Brazil the lead and Jairzinho followed up with a double to finish the game.

Brazil's next match was against the world champions: England. Only one goal was scored in the game, but it was a classic nonetheless. Brazil's supreme attacking talent came up against a magnificent defence, Pelé leading his compatriots against a defiant Bobby Moore, who time after time would break up Brazil's attacks. Pelé could draw out the best of his opponents, it would seem. Indeed, he did just that when Gordon Banks stopped Pelé opening the scoring with a stop dubbed the 'save of the century'. Carlos Alberto played a cutting pass from deep, allowing Jairzinho to get behind the England defence. He made it to the byline and crossed to Pelé, who headed powerfully towards the bottom corner. It looked as if the header was already beyond Banks as he reached behind him and tipped the ball up over the bar.

WORLD CUP LEGENDS

But Pelé and Brazil were not to be denied. They kept coming, and in the 59th minute, broke England's resolve. Tostão danced into the edge of the England box and lifted the ball into the middle. Pelé killed it dead with a deft touch, then shifted it outside into the path of Jairzinho to power home into the top corner.

Brazil's final group game was against Romania. They rested a couple of stars, shifting Gerson and Rivelino to the bench, but Pelé remained, and would again have a key role to play. He opened the scoring after 19 minutes with an inswinging free kick, and added another in the 67th minute in a 3-2 victory that took Brazil into the quarter-finals.

Brazil ploughed through their opposition in the knockout stages. First to fall were Peru, Pelé assisting a goal for Tostão in a 4-2 win. Pelé created another in Brazil's next match, a semi-final against Uruguay that they won 3-1, and where one of Pelé's most famous moments took place. As Pelé raced to meet a through ball, Uruguay's goalkeeper rushed out to try and snuff out the attack. Just as Pelé and the ball met the keeper at the edge of the box, Pelé feinted as if he was going to collect the ball and try to round the keeper. Instead, he left the ball untouched, passing the bamboozled keeper on one side, the ball on the other. Pelé over-rotated after collecting the ball at a wide angle and sent his shot wide of the far post, but the moment is still remembered as a great illustration of Pelé's footballing brilliance, despite the miss.

The final of the 1970 World Cup took place at the Azteca Stadium in Mexico City. Brazil met their antithesis, an Italy side known for its 'Catenaccio', or 'door-bolt', defensive system. It was a game that, perhaps more than any other, would cement Pelé's legend. Fittingly, it was Pelé who opened the scoring in the 18th minute with a powerful header, the diminutive figure rising high in the air to beat his taller marker. Italy found a way back into the game through Boninsegna on 37 minutes, exploiting a loose pass at the back. It stayed 1-1 going into half-time. Gerson took Brazil back into the lead with a powerful long-range drive in the 66th minute, and was again involved for Brazil's third, sending a long ball floating into the opposition box. Pelé was there to meet the pass with the perfect cushioned header sent back across goal into the path of an onrushing Jairzinho to give Brazil a 3-1 lead. Brazil then signed off with a goal that epitomised the flowing attacking football that had made this 1970 team such a pleasure to watch. It was the perfect final flourish to cap off a phenomenal tournament, and a goal that was truly worthy of a World Cup final. Indeed, it would go down in history as one of the greatest team goals ever scored.

The move started after Brazil won the ball deep in their own half. After an exchange of passes, the ball ended up with Clodoaldo at the base of midfield. He danced his way past four Italian players to the delight of the crowd, and then laid the ball off to Rivelino on the left side of the pitch at the halfway line. Rivelino played the ball forward to Jairzinho, who had drifted over from the right flank. Pelé later said that this was a deliberate ploy - Italy were employing a man-marking system, so Jairzinho would periodically drift over to pull Italy left back Giacinto Facchetti out of position, opening a space on the right they called 'the avenue'. After receiving Rivelino's pass, Jairzinho cut inside and laid the ball off to Pelé in the middle off the pitch. He paused for a moment, holding the ball up while he waited for the right moment to release it. Then he nonchalantly slid the ball out onto the right, into 'the avenue' Jairzinho vacated and ran into the path of an onrushing Carlos Alberto. Alberto crowned the move by smashing the ball low into the far corner. The final ended 4-1. Attack beat defence. Beauty triumphed over austerity.

The 1970 trophy was Brazil's third, making them the most successful team in World Cup history. They cemented their status as a premier football nation, and did it with the characteristic style that made 'Brazilian' a byword for skill, technique and flair. Pelé was recognised as the star of that unbelievably talented team, and awarded the Golden Ball for player of the tournament. It was Pelé's last World Cup, and the perfect end for his special relationship with the competition.

The beautiful football with which the 1970 Brazil team wowed the world should give us cause to remember that the legend of Pelé should not overshadow the talents of his teammates. Players like the great Garrincha, who played alongside Pelé in 1958 and led his nation to World Cup glory in 1962 in Pelé's absence. Or the phenomenal Jairzinho, who scored in every game of the 1970 tournament. Yet, while recognising their greatness, it is telling that even among all that gifted talent, Pelé's teammates and rivals revered him as the best. He is the most complete player football has ever seen, and he is unquestionably the World Cup's greatest icon. He gave the tournament some of its greatest moments and, in return, it gave him his.

PELÉ

○ The 1970 World Cup-winning Brazil team would go down as one of the greatest in history

BREAKING NEW FRONTIERS

Pelé is credited as a pioneer in helping to grow football in the US. He originally retired from club football after the 1974 season, though he would continue to make the odd appearance for Santos.

In 1975, Pelé officially came out of retirement to join the New York Cosmos. This was not Pelé at his peak, but he was still enough of a star to bring a lot of public interest to the young North American Soccer League, the precursor to Major League Soccer. The club's increased profile led them to move from a sparse pitch that the club's groundsman spray-painted green to hide the lack of grass for Pelé's debut on TV in the Yankee Stadium.

By Pelé's final season in 1977, the Cosmos averaged crowds of around 40,000, which was by far the biggest in the league. In that year, Pelé, alongside new signing Carlos Alberto and Germany legend Franz Beckenbauer, led the Cosmos to the NASL championship.

WORLD CUP LEGENDS

TOP 10: SCORERS

They shoot, and they really do score. Here we take a look at the World Cup's all-time leading goalscorers

LIONEL MESSI

Messi first stepped onto the World Cup stage back in 2006 when he came off the bench against Serbia and Montenegro. In a sign of things to come he slotted home a goal on his tournament debut in a 6-0 rout. He has since played in five World Cups, scoring 13 goals in 26 games, including a brace in the 2022 final, which Argentina won on penalties.

HELMUT RAHN

The most important of Rahn's 10 goals in 10 World Cup tournament matches came against Hungary in 1954 – the one that sealed World Cup glory for West Germany. He also helped his country to the semi-finals in the 1958 World Cup, a tournament that saw him become joint second goalscorer with Pelé on six goals.

JÜRGEN KLINSMANN

Klinsmann was a constant fixture during the 1990s, with appearances at the 1990, 1994 and 1998 World Cups – first for West Germany, and then for the unified German team. He scored in each tournament, getting 11 goals in total. He also picked up a World Cup winners' medal in 1990, and went on to manage Germany to third place in 2006.

KYLIAN MBAPPÉ

How do you top scoring four goals in your first World Cup and becoming only the second teenager to find the net in a final? By netting a hat-trick in your second World Cup final of course. With 12 goals in 14 games, Mbappé is a goal-scoring machine, one surely set to break the all-time record given he is still only 24 at the time of writing.

SÁNDOR KOCSIS

A key part of the famed Mighty Magyars side of the 1950s, Kocsis was ridiculously prolific for club and country. He netted an extraordinary 75 goals in 68 appearances for Hungary, including a remarkable 11 times at the 1954 World Cup in Switzerland. The first player to bag two hat-tricks in a single World Cup, only Just Fontaine has ever scored more in a single tornament.

TOP 10: SCORERS

PELÉ

⚽ **Pelé played in four World Cups: 1958, 1962, 1966 and 1970.** But what is perhaps most incredible is that he won all but one of them (1966), making him the only player to have lifted the World Cup three times. He scored 12 goals in 14 matches. Remarkably six of those goals came in 1970 after he had initially refused to take part.

JUST FONTAINE

⚽ **Fontaine played in just one tournament: 1958.** But what a time he had, sticking a staggering 13 goals in the back of the net despite playing just six games. That tally of 2.17 goals per game is pipped only by Sándor Kocsis (on 2.20) and yet, like Kocsis' Hungary, it still wasn't enough for France to win the tournament.

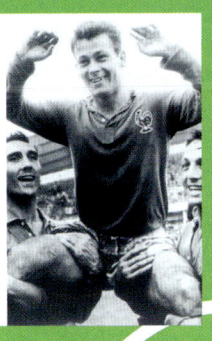

GERD MÜLLER

⚽ **Known as 'Der Bomber', Müller was stocky, robust and an absolute goal machine.** Smashing 68 goals in 62 games for West Germany, he secured the Golden Boot at the 1970 World Cup with 10 goals. Four years later in West Germany he found the net four times, helping the hosts to victory. He held the World Cup scoring record for 32 years.

RONALDO

⚽ **The Brazilian took part in four tournaments in 1994, 1998, 2002 and 2006.** He scored four in 1998, the year Brazil came runners-up to France, and he doubled that tally in 2002, scoring twice in the final. This not only got him a well-earned World Cup winners' medal, it cemented the Golden Boot award and won him man of the match too.

MIROSLAV KLOSE

⚽ **Klose competed in 2002, 2006, 2010 and 2014.** But although his five goals in that first tournament helped get Germany to the final, they lost to Brazil. There was further misery when they came third twice in a row. How thrilled he must have been to finally lift the World Cup in 2014 – in which he scored just two of his record-breaking 16 goals.

WORLD CUP LEGENDS

LEGENDS OF THE '66 WORLD CUP

It's 1966 and all that: relive the iconic extra-time victory that brought football back home, as told by those who were there

Within hours, London's *Evening Standard* had hit the streets. 'Champions of the World', ran the headline. "A dream come true. England have won the World Cup," it began. The following day, the Sunday newspapers also picked up the news, inevitably splashing it across their front pages: 'Golden Boys!' the *Sunday Mirror* proclaimed, before adding a chirpy note to the world's bankers: "Britain's reserves went up yesterday by one valuable gold cup." There was no doubt this would be a day to savour for decades to come.

On 30 July 1966, 96,924 people packed into Wembley Stadium and 32.3 million British viewers tuned in on their televisions to watch England take on West Germany in the World Cup final. Today, the names of the England players who took part that day can be reeled off one by one like old friends. But back then – despite Alf Ramsey declaring, "we will win the World Cup" when appointed England manager in 1962 – not many fans really believed they could do it.

"I don't think England supporters expect England to win anything and there was certainly that same feeling even back then," says West Ham fan John James, who attended the final in 1966. And yet Ramsey stuck to his word. He had formally taken charge on 1 May 1963, and promptly began to do things his way. The lack of control over team selections suffered by the previous manager, Walter Winterbottom, was not for him. Ramsey made his own choices, and whether that was naming Bobby Moore as England captain at just 22 years old, or playing without wingers in the face of disbelief, he stood by every decision he made.

As hosts, England automatically qualified for the 1966 FIFA World Cup, along with defending champions Brazil. That left 14

LEGENDS OF THE '66 WORLD CUP

Bobby Moore lifts the Jules Rimet trophy aloft in one of the most enduring images in English sporting history

WORLD CUP LEGENDS

other places which were taken by Argentina, Bulgaria, Chile, France, Hungary, Italy, North Korea, Mexico, Portugal, Spain, Switzerland, Uruguay, the Soviet Union and West Germany. All of England's games were held at Wembley and, while the team started slowly with a 0-0 draw against Uruguay, they then went on a sensational run of victories that took them straight to the final.

The night before the big day, Ramsey - with a nagging sense that the occasion could overwhelm his men - tried to help the players relax. Without fanfare, they went to watch *Those Magnificent Men in Their Flying Machines* at a local cinema. "Alf loved going to the pictures so we all strolled down to the picture house," recalls winger Terry Paine, who had just achieved promotion to the First Division with Southampton and played against Mexico in the second game. "And you know what? Not one photo was taken or autograph was asked. Can you imagine that today? You wouldn't get within 100 metres of anybody but that was a remarkable feature of football in those days."

It wasn't the first time Ramsey had tried to relieve anxieties among the squad. You could say it had become a speciality of his. After that group stage draw, he took the players to Pinewood Studios. "We mixed with stars such as Sean Connery and went on the set of the James Bond film," says Paine. "That was extra special and it got us over the disappointment." Ramsey treated the international side as if it were a club team. He adopted similar principles to those that had seen him turn Ipswich Town into league champions at the first time of asking. The team became close-knit and fostered a feeling of togetherness that would serve them well on the pitch.

On the eve of the final against West Germany, most of the talk concerned striker Jimmy Greaves and whether or not he would play in place of Geoff Hurst. For most of the tournament Greaves had partnered Roger Hunt up front, but an injury granted Hurst a

"I GOT TO THE DOOR OF THE DRESSING ROOM JUST AS BOBBY ARRIVED CARRYING THE GLEAMING JULES RIMET TROPHY"
Norman Giller, sports historian

○ The leather ball used in the 1966 World Cup final, originally claimed by West Germany's Helmut Haller

LEGEND OF MANAGEMENT: SIR ALF RAMSEY

What Alf Ramsey lacked in pace and height, he more than made up for with an uncanny knack for ensuring he was in the right part of the pitch at the right time. He made his professional debut on 26 October 1946 in a second division game for Southampton against Plymouth Argyle and proved himself to be an intelligent right-back. But after 96 appearances for the club, scoring eight goals, he left for Tottenham Hotspur and won the first division in 1951.

When his playing days were over, Ramsey went on to manage Ipswich Town in the Third Division (South) in 1955, leading them to promotion as champions. He won the first division with the club in 1961-62, an incredible success that led to him managing England. After winning the World Cup in 1966, he took England to third place in the UEFA European Championship in 1968 but quarter-final defeats at the 1970 World Cup and 1972 Euros, coupled with failure to qualify for the 1974 World Cup were disappointments that saw him sacked by the FA.

○ Ramsey was inducted as a manager into the English Football Hall of Fame in 2002 and again as a player in 2010

LEGENDS OF THE '66 WORLD CUP

George Cohen and Jack Charlton in action during the 1966 World Cup final

place in the team for the quarter-final. Hurst scored the only goal in that game and went on to provide an assist for Bobby Charlton in the semi. Unwilling to change a winning side, Ramsey decided to overlook Greaves for what would have been the biggest game of his life.

"Being a West Ham fan, I was pleased that Hurst was going to be involved in the final," says James. "The atmosphere for the games had also begun to change for the better. It had been quiet in the earlier rounds. For the final, there was a fabulous atmosphere. There were lots of Germans in the stadium - we were surprised at how many - but they were well outnumbered. It was something to behold."

Back then, the fans didn't wear replica kits. They just weren't available to buy. Neither did they fly the flag of St George, preferring the Union Flag instead. The supporters also turned up with their England rosettes proudly pinned to their clothes, swinging their rattles and making a tremendous noise. "It was very different to the guys with their drums and trumpets today," says Arsenal fan Roy O'Neil, who recalls buying his ticket from an agency at the Barbican in London for five times its face value, and ending up in a neutral zone of the stadium surrounded by Italian fans. "I remember the game being the first time I had heard the clapping routine which is still used today; the one that ends in the shout "England". It was unique at the time."

The game got underway at 3pm. England versus West Germany; Bobby Charlton pitted against Franz Beckenbauer; Bobby Moore marking the first victory in winning the coin toss and electing to kick off. The crowd were in high spirits and then, in the 12th minute, Helmut Haller cut the atmosphere completely dead. A cross from Sigfried Held was knocked from the head of Ray Wilson to his feet, allowing the German to fire a low cross-shot to Gordon Banks' right: 1-0 to West Germany. Just six minutes later, however, Moore sent a free kick flying over the German defence, into space created by Hurst. With a glancing header, he equalised.

England were playing tremendously well. "As a Liverpool fan, I was impressed with Hunt up front, or Sir Roger Hunt as he has always been known at Anfield," enthuses Dr Rogan Taylor, director of the Football Industry Group at the University of Liverpool. Hunt fired directly at the German goalkeeper Hans Tilkowski but just couldn't quite get it past. "The team were all playing their part and no one was letting the side down," says O'Neil.

But the crowd started to quieten as the minutes ticked away. "The fans didn't do much to lift the team at this point, I remember that quite starkly," says Manchester United fan John Toye. "But they began cheering again once Martin Peters scored to put England ahead again." It was the 78th

AFRICA PULLS OUT

Unfortunately, there were no sporting legends from Africa in the World Cup of 1966. Every team in the continent decided to pull out of the qualifiers in protest at the teams which topped the African zone having to play-off against European or Asian opposition for their place in the finals.

The feeling was that Africa should be offered a direct route for qualification, and the boycott led to the rules being changed for the 1970 tournament. One consequence of this action was that North Korea took part in the World Cup for the first time in 1966, which caused problems at home: the country wasn't recognised by the UK, and so it was almost refused entry. Today, five of the 32 finalists are taken from Africa.

WORLD CUP LEGENDS

"BOBBY MOORE WAS ONE OF THE GREATEST DEFENDERS THERE HAS BEEN … HE DIDN'T HAVE PACE BUT HIS SOCCER BRAIN WAS SECOND TO NONE"

Terry Paine, 1966 World Cup winner

minute and Peters shot from close range, having initially hit Horst-Dieter Höttges from a Hurst attempt.

With five minutes to go, the players who hadn't been selected to play in the team that day had assembled on the touchline on the orders of Ramsey and they were fully anticipating a win. They were all part of the team, Ramsey had told them, and so they must be supportive of those on the pitch. They waited for the referee to blow his whistle and then - drama.

In the 89th minute, moments after a narrowly wide shot by Charlton had England fans groaning, Wolfgang Weber shot towards the England goal. It crossed the line and the crowd went completely silent. "What a gut-wrencher at the stroke of full time," says James. It was 2-2 and that meant only one thing: an agonising extra 30 minutes. "No way did we think the team would win in extra time. The team was dejected but Alf came out, waved his finger and gave them a lecture." It seemed to do the trick.

The rest of the squad remained in situ for the duration of that half and, unlike James, Paine was confident. "I still believe Gordon Banks was the greatest goalkeeper the world has seen, he was a superstar," he says. "Bobby Moore was one of the best defenders there has ever been - he didn't have pace but his soccer brain was second to none. Ray Wilson could match Brazil's Garrincha for pace and Nobby Stiles was of the old school and did a great job. Martin Peters was an intelligent guy coming in from the left-hand side. Bobby Charlton speaks for himself. And young Alan Ball, the best one-touch player in the world. Then we had Geoff Hurst alongside the hard-working Roger Hunt."

Ball crossed to Hurst in the 101st minute and Hurst smashed the ball on the underside of the crossbar, causing it to bounce down on to the line and be cleared. But did it go in? Referee Gottfried Dienst consulted his linesman Tofiq Bahramov. "I remember him running over to this day," says Paine. "The Russian linesman said something which sounded like it would be 'yes'. The goal was given and from our point of view it was in."

The West Germans tried to rally but England were on a high. Some supporters ran on to the pitch and at home, viewers listened to a distracted Lancastrian BBC commentator named Kenneth Wolstenholme utter the infamous words: "Some people are on the pitch! They think it's all over!" Hurst blasted into the net and the crowd went wild. "It is now!" England had won the World Cup.

All across the country, people jumped in celebration. "I was only ten and watched it in our front room on our old battered black-and-white set while my mum went shopping," says Manchester United fan John Horne. "After the game, I went outside and repeatedly smashed

○ A beaming Queen Elizabeth presents Moore with the World Cup trophy following the game

the ball against our coal shed wall for the next three hours, imitating Geoff Hurst's winning goal." The result meant so much to so many people and enthusiasm for football soared among the population.

As Haller sneaked away with the match ball, whipping it from under Hurst's nose as he celebrated his hat-trick, the celebrations continued in the dressing room. "I got to the door of the England dressing room just as Bobby arrived carrying the gleaming, real Jules Rimet trophy", says sports historian and former *Daily Express* chief football reporter Norman Giller, who recalled the entire day in a comprehensive book called *July 30 1966:* *Football's Longest Day*. "All the England players were in a state of exhaustion as they pushed their way down the tunnel, yet Bobby looked immaculate without a bead of sweat."

Giller went to hug the captain in congratulation of the feat but Alf Ramsey appeared, irked by the disputed goal, and the journalist knew it was time to leave. Ramsey's spirit quickly lifted but the players were still in disbelief. "Will somebody pinch me," George Cohen was heard as saying. "Am I dreaming?" He wasn't. The players went to a reception at The Royal Garden in Kensington but the fans weren't ready to give up celebrating. As they got wind the players were at the luxury five-star hotel, they gathered outside, cheering as their new heroes appeared on the balcony.

The excitement lasted for weeks. Frank Wood, a reporter on the *Bolton Evening News*, recalled fans wanted to pay tribute to England's newest footballing legends. "There was one guy who twice walked the Pennine Way who suggested that all the stiles along the 250-mile route should be known as 'Nobbies'". That didn't happen but it didn't matter. The players had secured their place in history; the most successful England side of all time. "To win a World Cup, you need at least five world-class players," says Paine. "We probably had more than that." Result.

LOSING THE WORLD CUP

Although England achieved success in 1966, they actually managed to lose the World Cup – in the most literal sense. The trophy was stolen on the afternoon of 20 March 1966 from the Methodist Central Hall in Westminster where it had been put on display. It led to a nationwide hunt and much embarrassment for the FA but it also heralded another sporting legend: Pickles, a black-and-white collie, who sniffed out the Jules Rimet Trophy seven days later wrapped in a newspaper in a hedge in London.

"It was all over the news because there was this mystery element to it", recalls screenwriter Michael Chaplin, who based the TV drama, *Pickles: The Dog Who Won the World Cup*, on the story in 2006. "It was almost like a classic Ealing comedy – this ridiculous event whereby this iconic piece of silverware was taken and no one knew who did it. I thought it was charming; a British caper which lent itself well to an entertaining film."

WORLD CUP LEGENDS

MOMENTS

23 JULY 1966

EUSÉBIO NETS FOUR

One of the all-time greats stakes his claim as a World Cup legend

Whenever the conversation about the greatest footballers of all time comes up, it's only a matter of time before someone mentions Eusébio. His performance in the 1966 World Cup is one example of why. The Portugal striker was already a star coming into the tournament, having won the Ballon d'Or in 1965, and he would continue to show his pedigree while visiting the shores of host nation England.

The Black Panther was on characteristically lethal form, netting three goals for Portugal in the group stages to help them to wins over Hungary, Bulgaria and Brazil. In his team's quarter-final against North Korea, however, he really stepped up to the plate. Portugal looked like they were going to get knocked out of the tournament by underdogs North Korea after going 3-0 down within 25 minutes. Instead, Eusébio dragged them out of trouble, netting four consecutive goals in a phenomenal performance and leading his team to a 5-3 victory.

For two of his goals, Eusébio used his pace to latch onto balls played into the box, and finished emphatically, one of which was a particularly tasty effort placed perfectly in the top corner. Either side of his third goal were two converted penalties, both put away confidently and comfortably. Eusébio would add to his four-goal haul in Portugal's next game when he scored against England. However, they lost that game 2-1, and were eliminated. Eusébio finished as the tournament's top scorer with nine goals.

WORLD CUP LEGENDS

MARACANAZO:
A 'NATIONAL CATASTROPHE' FOR BRAZIL

Before winning five World Cups, Brazil suffered a trauma it can neither forget nor truly confront

"Everywhere has its irremediable national catastrophe, something like a Hiroshima. Our catastrophe, our Hiroshima, was the defeat by Uruguay in 1950."

This insight into the Brazilian national psyche offered by the late Nelson Rodrigues, one of the country's most distinguished playwrights, is a useful one for non-Brazilians.

How does one explain what was seen immediately after the Seleção's humiliating 7-1 defeat to Germany in the semi-final of the 2014 World Cup? If it had happened to England at Wembley, or to the French at the Stade de France, you might expect stunned silence and perhaps even some booing. But on 8 July 2014, the Mineirão stadium in Belo Horizonte was the picture of collective grief. Television cameras captured images of fans weeping in the stands, eyes skyward, while the men in yellow jerseys sank to their knees.

The first thing to understand is that Brazilians had been through it already, before the world had ever heard of Neymar, Ronaldo or even Pelé.

MARACANAZO

Brazil were heavy favourites for the tournament of 1950, the first World Cup in 12 years due to war in Europe. Not only did Brazil boast some of the world's best attackers, but they were also the hosts.

The home team played all but one of its matches at the new Maracanã stadium, which had been specially built for the tournament. Construction had been hit with severe delays, meaning matches kicked off as work was still being done to the new hulking monolith.

According to contemporary reports, concrete rained from its roof during a 21-gun salute in the opening ceremony. Nonetheless, the Maracanã was looked upon with immense pride in Brazil, a country which strove to challenge Europe's sporting hegemony. It was a politically important moment for Brazil too.

The government of the day, led by President Eurico Gaspar Dutra, believed that a home World Cup win would unite the population behind his often tumultuous regime and portray the rapidly industrialising country as a new world power.

Although they had never won a World Cup before, Brazilians were confident of their footballing pedigree and were unafraid of hype. The new footballing philosophy, distinct from those of European nations and neighbouring Argentina and Uruguay, was also beginning to take form.

Later termed 'jogo bonito', the style emphasised free-scoring attacking play and eschewed the more underhanded - and perhaps nasty - elements of traditional South American football. They had won the previous

> **"FOR US BRAZILIANS, IT WAS A MARK THAT STAYED, WHICH NO ONE CAN ERASE"**
> **CARLOS ALBERTO**

year's South American Championship, the precursor to the Copa América, at a canter, scoring almost six goals a game.

The Seleção duly raced through qualification for the 1950 World Cup's second phase. Scoring eight goals and conceding just two in three matches, Brazil topped their opening group, which also featured Yugoslavia, Switzerland and Mexico.

Although the format of the World Cup has been changed countless times over the decades, the 1950 tournament remains the only one for which the winners were not decided by a final knockout match. Rather, the destination of the Jules Rimet trophy would come down to a round robin between group winners Brazil, Sweden, Spain and Uruguay.

Buoyed by their encouraging early tournament performances, the home side raised their level by several gears for the final group stage. Sweden and Spain were dispatched 7-1 and 6-1 respectively, with forwards Ademir and Chico running riot.

The final group match was to be played against Uruguay, who had already beaten Sweden but were held to a 2-2 draw by Spain. Brazil knew a draw at the Maracanã would see

The Brazil team of 1950 lines up before their World Cup clash with Mexico, which they won 4-0

Moacir Barbosa, the Brazilian goalkeeper, carried the blame for the defeat for the rest of his life

Uruguay's victorious side of 1950 won their country's second World Cup following the triumph on home soil in 1930

THE MAN WHO DIED TWICE

In the aftermath of the Maracanazo defeat it was Brazil's three black players – Moacir Barbosa and defenders Bigode and Juvenal – who took the majority of the flak.

Despite being considered one of the world's greatest goalkeepers, Barbosa was made to suffer more than anyone else.

Roundly blamed by fans and journalists for an error that allowed Alcides Ghiggia to score Uruguay's winner, he would play only once again for his country.

When the Maracanã installed new goalposts in the 1960s the old wooden ones were given to Barbosa. His decision to burn them did little to exorcise his demons; his reputation as Brazil's bogey man haunted him for the rest of his life.

Barbosa once recalled that in 1970, the year in which the country won its third World Cup, he noticed a mother point him out in the street, telling her child that he was "the man who made all of Brazil cry".

Barbosa was even reportedly barred from visiting a national team training camp near Rio de Janeiro in 1993 ahead of a World Cup year. Administrators apparently feared he would bring the players bad luck.

Speaking to a journalist shortly before his death in 2000, Barbosa said, "In Brazil, the most you get for any crime is 30 years. For 50 years I've been paying for a crime I did not commit. Even a criminal when he has paid his debt is forgiven. But I have never been forgiven. I am not guilty. There were 11 of us."

MARACANAZO

An emotional Brazil fan reacts to the 7-1 defeat by Germany during the 2014 World Cup

them crowned world champions. According to estimates, just under 200,000 fans - or about a tenth of the population of Rio de Janeiro - piled into the ground to witness Brazil's presumed coronation.

Such was the local confidence that a samba band stood pitch-side throughout the Uruguay match, ready to play a new song - *Brazil the Winners* - on the full-time whistle.

A number of local newspapers, assuming nothing would go wrong, even began calling the side the 'Champions of the World', while Rimet, the then-FIFA President for whom the World Cup trophy was named, prepared a congratulatory speech in Portuguese.

Incredibly, 22 gold medals, each one inscribed with the names of each Brazilian squad member, had reportedly already been made, while the mayor of Rio de Janeiro delivered a rousing pre-match speech in which he "already saluted the team as victors".

Alcides Ghiggia, Uruguay's star winger, later said, "It was a fantastic atmosphere. Their supporters were jumping with joy as if they'd already won the World Cup.

"Everyone was saying they'd thrash us three or four nil. I tried not to look at the crowd and just to get on with the match."

Brazil began more brightly than their southern neighbours, imposing themselves on the match and creating a number of chances. Although the first half ended 0-0, the home side found themselves a goal up just two minutes into the second period.

However, their lead only lasted until the 66th minute, Ghiggia getting the best of his marker to find a yard of space before whipping in a fierce delivery that was steered home by Juan Alberto Schiaffino. Uruguay had equalised, and they soon found themselves on the front foot.

With just over ten minutes remaining, the diminutive Ghiggia picked up the ball once more and hurtled down the wing and into the Brazilian penalty area. He shaped to cross, as he had done countless times that afternoon. Preparing to meet the delivery, Moacir Barbosa, the Brazilian goalkeeper, moved a fraction towards the centre of his goal, leaving a crack of space open between himself and his near post. Ghiggia spotted the chance and rifled a low right-footed shot into the net via the post. He would later comment that, "Three people have silenced the Maracanã - Frank Sinatra, the Pope and me."

With Brazil unable to find an equaliser Uruguay were crowned World Cup champions for the second time. Despair swept the ground like wildfire. Tales later emerged of a number of distraught fans spontaneously taking their own lives by leaping from the stands.

Arthur Nemesio, a Brazilian fan who attended the match, described the scene to *The Guardian* in 2014,: "There were a lot of people crying. A lot of men, women, boys, girls crying. It was the saddest day in the history of Brazilian football."

It's hard to overstate the collective impact of the 1950 World Cup on Brazil. Five subsequent World Cup wins have failed to expunge the memory of the match, forever known as Maracanazo, and it is commonplace for Brazilians to refuse to discuss it openly.

Carlos Alberto, a Brazilian World Cup winner in 1970, once said that the failure to win on home soil will always haunt his country.

"We had the chance to win," he said. "It's always important to win at home, like England won in 1966, like Germany won in 1974, like Argentina won in 1978. For us Brazilians, it was a mark that stayed, which no one can erase."

Yet out of the misery a new steeliness was born in Brazilian football, as were the Seleção's iconic canary-yellow jerseys. The white strips the team had worn in defeat to Uruguay would never be seen again after 1953.

Pelé later said one of his earliest memories were of his father's tears after the Maracanazo. "My father told me that you have to win the World Cup for Brazil," he said. In Sweden eight years later, aged just 17, he would do just that.

45

WORLD CUP LEGENDS

TOP 10: KEEPERS

It's not often that goalkeepers are the hero – so often they find themselves the villain – so here's 10 of the very best to have graced the world stage

HOPE SOLO

A runner-up in 2011, Solo went one better in 2015 as the USA clinched their third title. Conceding only three goals during the entire tournament, Solo made critical saves in a 3-1 win over Australia and distracted Germany's Célia Šašić to such an extent that she missed her semi-final spot kick.

JOSÉ LUIS CHILAVERT

Goalkeepers have a reputation for being frustrated outfield players, and Chilavert could not be caged. None of his eight international goals came at a World Cup, but he was the first keeper to take a direct free kick at the competition, almost scoring against Bulgaria.

NADINE ANGERER

Of all the keepers to play in a World Cup, Angerer boasts the best record. Winning the tournament in 2003 without playing a minute, her time to shine came four years later. This time not missing a minute of the action, Angerer didn't concede a single goal (a record of 540 minutes) and saved a Marta penalty in the final as Germany won 2-0.

FABIEN BARTHEZ

Laurent Blanc used to kiss his goalkeeper's bald head for good luck before every game – and in 1998 it seemed to work. His five clean sheets helped France to a famous home victory, and his 10 shutouts in 17 appearances are a World Cup record, shared with Peter Shilton.

DINO ZOFF

At 40, Zoff was the oldest man to win the World Cup when he captained Italy to glory in 1982. Despite his age, his reflexes left nothing to be desired: his late save from Oscar in a quarter-final against Brazil was one of the greats.

TOP 10: KEEPERS

LEV YASHIN

Not many men can claim to have revolutionised the position of goalkeeper, but 'The Black Spider' was among the first to marshal his defence rather than merely block the ball. He also played in four World Cups for the Soviet Union and won the Ballon d'Or in 1963.

GIANLUIGI BUFFON

'Gigi' seems to embody everything that is great about the World Cup. A fiercely proud Italian, he is the most capped player in his country's history, and in 2006 topped the world while conceding no goals from open play and being chosen as goalkeeper of the tournament, then the Yashin Award.

IKER CASILLAS

The Casillas home has quite the trophy cabinet, but among five Spanish league titles, three Champions Leagues and two European Championships, one medal has pride of place: the 2010 World Cup winners' medal. Not only that, but he was the man to lift the trophy as captain.

GORDON BANKS

Apart from winning the 1966 World Cup, Banks is also responsible for one of the greatest saves in the tournament's history. In a game that would decide Group 3, Brazil legend Pelé nodded the ball downwards towards the bottom corner of the goal, only to be stunned when Banks leapt across to divert it behind for a corner.

OLIVER KAHN

No goalkeeper had ever won the Golden Ball before Kahn's triumph in 2002. Twice Kahn brilliantly denied Robbie Keane in a group stage clash and in the last-16 fixture against Paraguay, Kahn produced at least one and perhaps two world-class saves in a 1-0 win. And in the final, the imperious Ronaldo might have had four had it not been for Kahn.

WORLD CUP LEGENDS

MARTA: THE GREATEST OF ALL TIME

A footballing warrior who travelled hundreds of miles in pursuit of her dream

Marta Vieira de Silva grew up being told that she wasn't normal. Neighbours in the small town of Dois Riachos in Brazil where she was raised would tell her mother that girls didn't play football, and they would do all they could to discourage her. It was a struggle that she would reflect upon in 2017 in a lengthy open note called *Letter to My Younger Self*. The fact that the world knows her simply as Marta, however, tells its own story.

In truth, Marta is not normal. Far from it. Rather, this creative centre-forward is very special indeed. Dubbed 'Pelé in a skirt' - a nickname often seized upon by the media but one that actually jars since she needs no comparison - Marta is arguably the most talented female footballer to have ever graced a pitch. She was named FIFA World Player of the Year five consecutive times between 2006 and 2010. In 2018, she won it for a sixth time, aged 32.

In many ways she is testament to the fact that great talent will, eventually, find a way of reaching the top through sheer perseverance, self-recognition and an innate belief. Having grown up playing football from the age of seven, competing against boys in the streets and using folded up plastic bags as a ball if there wasn't a proper one around, no one could have blamed her if she had given up. The fact she didn't and instead raised her game, even though it often led to resentment against her, is truly admirable. But then Brazil's treatment of the women's game as a whole had historically been harsh.

Even though ten women's football clubs had been flourishing in Rio de Janeiro in 1940, the then Brazilian president Getúlio Vargas allowed a decree to be drafted the following year that ensured women "will not be allowed to practice sports incompatible with the conditions of their nature". It ended up banning women's football until 1979, and the gender stereotypes that it helped to spawn continued apace.

Yet Marta, who was born on 19 February 1986, pushed against the ongoing prejudice. She gained a place on a five-aside indoor team and got over the controversy of an opponent team's coach declaring he'd pull his side from a regional cup tournament if Marta played. Aged 14, she was discovered by the Brazilian coach Helena Pacheco and, following a spell in the youth team for Centro Sportivo Alagoano, a team based in the city of Maceió, she moved to Vasco de Gama football club in Rio de Janeiro in 2000. It took a three-day bus journey to get there, but her professional career had begun, and she secured 16 appearances and four goals over two seasons.

Marta's skill with the ball was evident. Her dribbling skills were perfect and suitably inspired by the style of football Brazil has become infamous for over many decades. Meanwhile, her fast pace, ability to think quickly and outwit opponents were also emerging. A lack of funding for Vasco de Gama's women's team led to it being disbanded, but she continued her career at Santa Cruz Futebol Clube and, perhaps most notably, she excelled in the 2002 FIFA U-19 Women's World Championship.

Standout games included a 4-0 drubbing of France by Brazil on 21 August, during which she scored a hat-trick. She then netted twice in a 4-3 quarter-final win over Australia before scoring again in a 1-1 semi-final draw against Canada. While Brazil ultimately finished fourth overall having suffered two penalty shootout defeats, Marta had made a major breakthrough on the world stage despite being only 16 years

○ Marta went from playing in the streets against boys without shoes to starring on the world stage

WORLD CUP LEGENDS

WARM WELCOME FOR A HERO

To make it as a footballer, Marta had to leave Dois Riachos, the tiny city to the west of the Brazilian state of Alagoas. Yet Dois Riachos did not entirely leave her. While she went around the world showcasing her speedy dribbling skills, strong left foot and penchant for creating chances for teammates, people back home were taking their most famous star to their hearts, despite the negativity of those around her growing up.

Indeed, in Marta's *Letter to My Younger Self*, she writes of going back to her place of birth after winning the FIFA World Player of the Year award for the first time in 2006, and she tells her 14-year-old self to expect "crowds of people welcoming you home".

"Everyone wants to see the hometown hero who's come back," she adds. "They'll even drive you around in a fire truck. You won't be rejected anymore. The same people who said you were odd, that you couldn't play – that you shouldn't play – will be applauding as you go by." Such admiration continues today, with fans queuing for photographs with her whenever they're able to seize an opportunity. As one of the most recognisable stars of the game today, the widespread adoration for Marta is sure to continue for some time yet.

○ Fans grab photos on their phones during the men's football final at the 2016 Olympic Games in Rio de Janeiro

---

old. As a consequence she went to the 2003 Pan American Games and helped Brazil win Gold, scoring twice in the group stages and twice in the semi-final against Argentina. More than that, however, she was called up to the Brazil squad for the 2003 Women's World Cup.

Marta was 17 yet unfazed by the attention she was getting. She ended up filling in for the acclaimed but injured attacking midfielder Sissi. Wearing the number 10 shirt, she coolly scored a penalty in the 14th minute of her first game against South Korea, which the Brazilians won 3-0. Awarded player of the match, she then went on to score against Norway in a 4-1 victory and netted another penalty in the 2-1 quarter-final defeat to Sweden on 1 October before a crowd of 25,103 at the Gillette Stadium in Foxboro, US. Her reputation as a playmaker was blossoming, and she not only played in a manner beyond her years but drove her team's performance by laying on great balls and dictating the run of the game. Little wonder Umeå IK of Sweden snapped her up in 2004.

Marta played for Umeå IK for four glorious seasons, making 103 appearances and scoring a magnificent 111 goals. During that spell she won the UEFA Women's Cup, the league four times and the Swedish Cup once. But, as well as taking part in the Pan American Games of 2007 (scoring two penalties to assist in beating the US 5-0 to take gold), she also made a second World Cup appearance.

Taking place in China, this World Cup almost belonged to Marta, who was by now truly getting into her stride. Aged just 21, she scored twice in the opening match against New Zealand and twice against China in 5-0 and 4-0 victories respectively. She also slotted home a penalty in a 3-2 win over Australia and two in the semi-final against the United States. All of this earned Marta the Golden Shoe for her seven goals, and the Golden Ball for being best player of the tournament, only for Germany to lift the World Cup. Even crueller was her missed penalty in that game, Germany's goalkeeper Nadine Angerer deflecting her potentially equalising shot wide.

Still, her star was on the rise, and a couple of years after that tournament Marta made a Hollywood-esque move to the US, signing for the Women's Professional Soccer club Los Angeles Sol, a deal that marked the league's inaugural season. She made 19 appearances and scored ten goals for the club before showing her stamina by going on loan to Santos during the US off-season for three months (scoring in the finals of the Copa Libertadores de Fútbol Femenino and the Copa do Brasil de Futebol Feminino, winning both titles). Sol then closed in January 2010 and Marta went to play for FC Gold Pride, a club in Santa Clara, California. There she won the WPS Championship.

Although Marta would then briefly return to Santos before moving to Western New York Flash in 2011 (the latter providing another WPS Championship), all eyes were on what she could do at the FIFA Women's World Cup that year. Again, Marta performed well and victories against Australia, Equatorial Guinea

> ## "SHE COOLLY SCORED A PENALTY IN THE 14TH MINUTE OF HER FIRST GAME AGAINST SOUTH KOREA"

○ Servet Uzunlar and Tameka Butt of Australia attempt to close Marta down in the 2011 FIFA Women's World Cup

MARTA

Marta endured a frustrating 2023 World Cup. Brazil's group-stage exit was a sad way for her time on the biggest stage to (likely) end

and Norway (against who she scored two) proved relatively easy.

Unfortunately, Brazil came unstuck in the quarter-finals against the United States despite Marta scoring twice, once from the penalty spot. She scored another from the spot when the game went to extra time and ended in a shoot-out. Yet while the US ultimately progressed at Brazil's expense, Marta at least finished with the Silver Boot and a well-deserved place in the tournament's All-Star Team. What perhaps proved more jarring were the loud boos from opponent fans. Her talent was clearly inspiring jealousy once more. Not that it unduly affected her.

In 2012 she signed for Tyresö FF in Sweden on a salary of $400,000 per season and won another league title. She then went on to sign for Swedish rivals FC Rosengård in 2014, winning the league twice more, along with the Svenska Supercupen. Such was her unwavering fitness, agility and undoubted skill that she found herself in the squad for the next World Cup, her fourth.

In that tournament Brazil beat South Korea 2-0 in the opening game, Marta's penalty becoming a record 15th World Cup goal. Sadly for her it was the only one she'd score as Brazil crashed out in the quarter-finals.

Once again the world had been denied the sight of a great talent plying her trade on the greatest of stages. Instead fans were left to reflect on the past – of that time in 2007, perhaps, when she got past a defender with a back heel, spiralled around another and smashed the ball into the net. Even Neymar had called Marta the best in the world in 2015, but defeat there means Marta has still never won a World Cup (although she does have three Copa América Femeninas from 2003, 2010 and 2018 to her name).

The 2019 World Cup in France provided Marta with another opportunity to go all the way with Brazil, and once again she proved crucial, burying her second penalty of the tournament in a 1-0 group-stage victory over Italy to secure a spot in the knockout stages. Unfortunately for Brazil, the hosts awaited them in the next round. After a tense 90 minutes finished at 1-1, extra time loomed, during which France snatched a winner to send Brazil crashing out.

Further disappointment came in 2020 when, despite Marta becoming the first female player to score at five consecutive Olympics by finding the net against China (and later the Netherlands), Brazil fell to eventual champions Canada on penalties.

Returning to the domestic scene with Orlando Pride, Marta focused on her club career, having left FC Rosengård in 2017 for free after the club had agreed to terminate her contract. She settled into life in the US well, but then, in March 2022, injury struck.

Leaping to contest an aerial duel during a narrow cup defeat to North Carolina, Marta landed awkwardly, and it would later transpire that she had suffered knee ligament damage that would require surgery to rectify. Not only would she miss the rest of the domestic season, but her injury would also rule her out of the 2022 Copa América Femenina, which Brazil utterly dominated, scoring 20 goals and conceding none en route to an eighth continental title.

Determined to represent Brazil on the biggest stage once more, Marta flew out to the 2023 World Cup (which was co-hosted by Australia and New Zealand) harbouring hopes of one final shot at the game's greatest prize. Sadly, it wasn't to be, with the Canaries crashing out in the group stages in what was most likely Marta's last World Cup.

Regardless of whether she returns in 2027, her place in the pantheon of greats has long been assured. There'll be other stars, but there'll only ever be one Marta.

WORLD CUP LEGENDS

MOMENTS
7 JUNE 1970

TWO ICONS SWAP SHIRTS

Brazil's Pelé and England's Bobby Moore swap shirts in a famous show of respect

The 1970 World Cup was host to one of the competition's finest games, a match between the World Cup holders at the time, England, and arguably the greatest World Cup side ever fielded, the 1970 Brazil team. The game's close also provided us with one of the World Cup's most iconic images, when Brazil legend Pelé swapped shirts with England captain Bobby Moore.

The match itself was closely fought, Gordon Banks' most famous save denying Pelé a goal when he flicked his header up over the bar, and England squandering several good chances. One of the key features of the game was the battle between the incredible attacking talent of Brazil - the likes of Jairzinho, Rivelino, Gerson and Pelé - and England's defence, led by Bobby Moore. The former came out on top, with Brazil getting a 1-0 victory.

After the final whistle, Pelé and Moore embraced, swapping shirts in a sign of mutual respect. The two clearly admired each other's talents - indeed, Pelé would later call Moore the best defender he ever faced - and the gesture was intended to acknowledge how good they each knew the other was after a competitive match. The warm smiles they both wore as they conversed led to the moment being praised as an example to follow as to the spirit in which the game should be played: two rivals who had given everything they had engaging with sportsmanship, dignity and friendship.

WORLD CUP LEGENDS

DIEGO MARADONA:
ARGENTINA'S GOLDEN BOY

Genius, saviour, cheat: Maradona has been called many things by many men, but he remains 'El Diego'

It would be quite possible, although not entirely plausible, to devote the entirety of this ode to El Diego to that one goal. No, not *that* goal, the other one. The second one. The decade-defining 11 seconds of brilliance that left the England team strewn across the field of the Azteca in the hot sun, wondering what they had to do to stop the little Argentinian. The truth was that they weren't the first, they wouldn't be the last, and few would ever find a solution.

Having taken his first professional bow as a 14 year old, it certainly did not take the national team long to recognise Diego Maradona's talents. He made his senior debut in 1977 at the age of 16, the youngest Argentinian international ever.

However, probably wisely given his later predilections for distraction, manager César Luis Menotti (known as 'El Flaco' - 'the slim one') did not pick him for the 1978 home World Cup because he felt he was too young. It didn't seem to hinder his side, who lifted the trophy after beating the Netherlands in the final.

When Maradona did make it to football's biggest show, he was a world away from the teenager whom El Flaco had left out.

But Barcelona pounced just before the rest of the world could see what Maradona was about. In 1982, he was sold for a world-record fee of nearly double what Boca had paid for him just 12 months previously. Perhaps if Barça had waited, they might have put their cheque book away again.

With Argentina playing their first game of Spain '82 at the Camp Nou against Belgium, the stage was quite perfectly set for the Argentinian to make good the disappointment of missing out in 1978 and simultaneously win over his new fans in Catalonia. He came within inches of a fairytale moment, a second-half free kick hitting the crossbar, but otherwise Argentina were stodgy and disappointing, going down 1-0. Maradona was greeted with a level of on-field aggression bordering on out-and-out violence.

The squad was uncomfortably tense, inside and out. Plenty of the experienced 1978 champions had been retained beyond usefulness and it had not gone unnoticed: Minotti was slammed in the Argentinian press for remaining loyal to older players and deploying the younger Maradona in a deeper role. They even questioned whether the Falklands conflict, which officially only ended the day after the defeat to Belgium, was affecting the players. (Maradona recalled that the Argentinian media had been largely censored with regards to the war and that when the team reached Spain, they read that they were very much losing a conflict they had been told they were winning.)

But better news was to follow for the Buenos Aires press - on the pitch at least. Maradona was virtuosic in the second match against Hungary, scoring his first two World Cup goals. That 4-1 win was followed by a 2-0 victory over El Salvador and in the second group stage, they returned to Catalonia.

But there was no redemption for Maradona, whom Italy defender Claudio Gentile repeatedly hacked down in a 2-1 win. The referee appeared unconcerned and even

> **"MARADONA WAS GREETED WITH A LEVEL OF ON-FIELD AGGRESSION BORDERING ON OUT-AND-OUT VIOLENCE"**

Maradona triumphantly holds the trophy after the 1986 World Cup final between Argentina and West Germany

DIEGO MARADONA

WORLD CUP LEGENDS

Maradona would see red against Brazil in 1982, with Argentina crashing out in the second round

booked Maradona, who was fouled a record 23 times in the game, for dissent. "Football is not for ballerinas," said the typically hard-nosed Gentile after the game.

Having already lost two of four games, the champions' clash with the imperious Brazil side was something of a foregone conclusion. Even the manner of it could be written ahead of time. And Maradona, full of four years of frustration at his own national side and three weeks of being kicked up and down the pitches of Spain, was unable to contain his frustration any longer. With Argentina trailing 3-0, Maradona aimed a kick at the ball and Brazilian midfielder Batista, who had just caught Argentina's Juan Barbas in the head with his studs. Maradona was promptly sent off. It was an unfair and ignominious end to his first World Cup. His new city booed him off the pitch. The disappointment only served to inspire Maradona to make his mark on the next tournament four years later.

Given that he had utterly failed to win over any Barça fans with his World Cup performances and perhaps even turned some against him, it is unsurprising that his two-year spell with the famous club was something of a struggle. Despite his 38 goals in 58 appearances, Maradona fell out with a number of senior figures at the club, contracted hepatitis, suffered a horrific ankle break that "sounded just like a piece of wood splitting" and developed a serious and persistent cocaine habit.

In the summer of 1984, Maradona broke the world transfer record again and headed to Napoli where, if he was not already developing a God complex, he would find ample ammunition. He was greeted by 75,000 adoring fans at the famous Stadio San Paolo. They immediately stripped club legend Giuseppe Bruscolotti of the captain's armband and gave it to Maradona. And when Argentina came to the 1986 World Cup in Mexico, the 25 year old was well and truly peaking.

Qualification had gone well. Maradona had scored three times and he had been made captain by manager Carlos Bilardo, a man whom he would come to call a mentor before a 2010 falling out.

The group draw pitted them against Italy, who had contributed to their downfall four years previously. After being publicly nullified by the violence of the 1982 World Cup, Maradona's growth in reputation had only served to ensure that teams would redouble

"WHEN ARGENTINA CAME TO THE 1986 WORLD CUP IN MEXICO, THE 25-YEAR-OLD MARADONA WAS WELL AND TRULY PEAKING"

THE HAND OF GOD

Maradona had started the move with typical flair in midfield before Jorge Valdano miscontrolled his pass, only for Steve Hodge to help the ball on its way towards goal. Maradona did the rest, punching the ball past England goalkeeper Peter Shilton with what Tunisian referee Ali Bin Nasser believed to be his head. It became an iconic moment.

Nasser's decision to allow Maradona's punched effort in the 1986 World Cup quarter-final haunted him for the rest of his career. He never refereed at a finals again and his efforts to blame linesman Bogdan Dochev turned into a slanging match, with each accusing the other. Maradona meanwhile, he later revealed, was hissing at his teammates to celebrate, because manager Carlos Bilardo had warned them not to celebrate any goals to save energy in the hot Mexican sun – but Maradona was worried that the unusual behaviour might alert the referee to the foul play.

In the post-match press conference, Maradona cheekily said the goal had been scored by the head of Maradona and "the hand of God", coining the phrase by which the controversial strike would become known. It intensified what was an already fierce footballing rivalry and Argentina seemed to relish the pain the controversy inflicted.

DIEGO MARADONA

○ After missing out on Argentina's 1978 World Cup victory, Maradona finally got his hands on the ultimate prize in 1986

WORLD CUP LEGENDS

Following wins over Greece and Nigeria in the 1994 World Cup, Maradona was banned from the tournament after testing positive for ephedrine

their efforts to injure him. Just as Pelé had been in 1966, Maradona was a marked man. He would go on to draw more fouls at that World Cup than any other player in history.

In the opening game of the tournament against South Korea, Maradona found himself tripped, kicked, pushed and even punched around the pitch. One player even managed to get his studs through Maradona's socks and bandaged legs to draw blood. Undeterred, and more used to the treatment after two years in the Italian league with Napoli, Maradona did not kick back. The South Koreans were beaten 3-1, with Maradona providing assists for all three goals.

Next came Italy, who did enough to take an early lead from the spot, only for Maradona to get on the scoresheet for the first time in the tournament, beating the keeper with a perfectly placed volley. The points were split and Argentina's 2-0 win over Bulgaria – Maradona only had a hand in one of the goals this time – was enough to send them through at the top of Group A. And once they had beaten South American neighbours Uruguay 1-0, in which FIFA had warned Uruguay about potential trouble in the game and duly quashed much of the physicality against Maradona for 90 minutes at least, they were pitted against England.

That game has had more written about it than perhaps any other. Four years after the Falklands War, this was the rematch that Argentina wanted with a rival they already had plenty of reasons to hate. But it is a testament to the quality of what followed that it can be remembered overwhelmingly for footballing reasons.

Generous commentators would call England's defence 'resolute' or 'single-minded', others would favour 'heavy-handed'. Terry Fenwick was immediately booked for an ugly foul on Maradona that seemed to set a standard for the game, and the Argentine star created a number of good chances that forced Peter Shilton into action. The warning signs were there and six minutes after the break, he skipped past four England players before Steve Hodge inadvertently chipped the ball towards his own goalkeeper, only for Maradona to punch the ball past him and into

DIEGO MARADONA

"MARADONA BEAT FOUR ENGLAND PLAYERS BEFORE SCORING ONE OF THE GREATEST GOALS IN WORLD CUP HISTORY"

the net. The referee thought it was a header. His was the only opinion that mattered.

While his first goal may have been controversial, his second was unforgettable. Four minutes after the first, in the space of 11 seconds, Maradona slalomed past Peter Reid, Terry Fenwick and Terry Butcher before beating Shilton with a feint and scoring one of the greatest goals in World Cup history.

For Argentina, that game was bigger than winning the World Cup. It was about avenging 'Las Malvinas' and sinking the English World Cup warship. For many fans, the rest of 1986 is a blur of Maradona skills. He gained more personal redemption for 1982 in the semi-finals, scoring two exquisite goals to reach the final. Once there, it looked as though Argentina would be able to seal victory without Maradona adding too much. West Germany's Lothar Matthäus was his shadow and while the odd pass and flick helped Argentina to a 2-0 lead, Maradona wasn't as integral as in previous rounds.

But in seven second-half minutes, the West Germans fought back to level the game and pushed on for a winner, desperate to avoid extra time in gruelling conditions. However, that allowed Maradona all the space he needed. Six minutes from time, with the Germans overextended in attack, he split the defence with a delicate pass and set Jorge Burruchaga free. Minutes later, Maradona was lifting the Jules Rimet Trophy and the Golden Ball, both richly deserved.

The only thing harder than winning the World Cup is retaining it. But in 1990, it looked as though Argentina might be about to do just that. By now, Maradona had led Napoli to two Serie A titles, a Coppa Italia and a UEFA Cup – but his off-field behaviour, particularly drug use, had never improved, although he had not yet failed a substance test.

Italy were the hosts, a country who had kicked Maradona out of the tournament eight years ago. But, for an already injury-ravaged Argentina squad, things started disastrously. They scraped through the group stages after a shock loss to Cameroon and were pitted against Brazil in the second round. With Maradona carrying an injury, another kicking ensued at the hands of their South American rivals. However he was still able, in the dying minutes, to produce a moment of quality, running through the Brazilian midfield before putting Claudio Caniggia through on goal.

Maradona's roller coaster World Cup continued in a shootout in the quarter-final: after failing to score against a Yugoslavian team who had ten men for 100 minutes, his tame shot was saved only for his teammates to spare his blushes and put them through. The semi-final against Italy went to penalties

MARADONA: THE MANAGER

It does not always ring true that the best players make the best managers. In fact, it often seems to be the opposite. Certainly, Maradona's lifestyle did not appear to be a natural fit with the job. His most prominent spell as a manager came from 2008 to 2010, when he took over the national side in Argentina – despite having not worked as a manager since that ill-fated mid-'90s spell. Unsurprisingly, it would prove a turbulent time.

His fourth game in charge saw Argentina equal their record defeat, a 6-1 loss to Bolivia that left them staring down the barrel of failing to qualify for the 2010 World Cup. But he rallied a side bursting with attacking talent – Sergio Agüero, Lionel Messi and Juan Román Riquelme were joint top-scorers for the side – to seal qualification… and promptly told the media to "suck it and keep sucking it" on live TV. A two-month ban and hefty fine followed.

The World Cup itself went swimmingly, with four straight wins before they were thrashed 4-0 by Germany in the quarter-finals. Maradona wanted to stay on, but was eventually sacked and accused national team director Carlos Bilardo of betraying him as a parting shot.

WORLD CUP LEGENDS

"MARADONA SOBBED HIS WAY THROUGH THE PRESENTATION CEREMONIES, A MAN WHOSE TALENT HAD BEGUN TO WANE"

too, but in front of his home Napoli crowd, Maradona stepped up to take the fourth spot kick, a carbon copy of his last except that it beat Walter Zenga and Argentina went through to the final where the mighty West Germany waited.

The Germans had lost two finals in a row, and with Maradona limping and Argentina stuttering, they would rarely get a better chance to make amends.

There was an acceptance in the media that at 29 years old, living as he did and with the injuries he had been through, Maradona was unlikely to play another World Cup. Already, his body was not the one that had led Argentina to victory in 1986. But those looking for a glorious exit to underline his place in the World Cup hall of fame were left sadly wanting that night in Rome.

It was known as one of the dirtiest finals in World Cup history, and would only be eclipsed in 2010 by the Battle of Johannesburg. Maradona had admitted beforehand that they, with four players suspended and he himself walking wounded, would need a miracle to turn over the Germans, and in truth it never looked likely. And it was rendered nigh-on impossible when substitute Pedro Monzón was sent off just after the hour mark. Andreas Brehme's 85th-minute penalty and Gustavo Dezotti's second yellow card only served to fulfil the inevitability of the result and absolve West Germany for the sins of two previous final defeats.

Maradona sobbed his way through the presentation ceremonies, a broken man whose mighty talent had begun to wane, crying for himself as much as anyone else.

But that was not to be the end of his World Cup story, although his 1994 appearance would be best forgotten. He had left Napoli under the cloud of a 15-month drugs ban - his cocaine habit had finally been caught out - and a one-year spell back with Carlos Bilardo

MARADONA FACTS & FIGURES

312 GOALS SCORED IN **590** PROFESSIONAL GAMES ACROSS THREE COUNTRIES

34 GOALS SCORED IN **91** INTERNATIONALS FOR ARGENTINA

16 MOST APPEARANCES AS CAPTAIN AT A WORLD CUP

GOLDEN BALL FIRST PLAYER EVER TO WIN THE GOLDEN BALL AT UNDER-20 AND SENIOR WORLD CUP – LIONEL MESSI IS THE ONLY ONE SINCE

23 FOULED MORE TIMES THAN ANY ONE PLAYER IN A WORLD CUP MATCH (23 TIMES VS ITALY AT SPAIN '82) AND IN ONE WORLD CUP (53 TIMES AT MEXICO '86)

21 STARTED 21 CONSECUTIVE MATCHES FOR ARGENTINA AT FOUR WORLD CUPS

24 BROKE THE WORLD TRANSFER RECORD TWICE BEFORE THE AGE OF 24

DIEGO MARADONA

Maradona scores one of the greatest goals in World Cup history against England in 1986

at Sevilla did not work out. His weight was ballooning, his behaviour more out of control and he had barely played for Argentina. But a new-look Argentina team, without Maradona, had ended up in a World Cup play-off against Australia just to qualify for USA '94 and the country begged for him to be picked. El Diego was happy to answer their prayers. He played little part in a 2-1 aggregate win, an Alex Tobin own goal proving the winner in Buenos Aires.

But the pressure proved too much. In February, he pulled out of the squad. However, he soon changed his mind and was handed the captaincy for the tournament. In the opening game, Maradona scored a goal filled with emotion. After a quick passing move with Greece already well beaten at 2-0 down, Maradona hammered the ball into the top corner. The image of him running towards the camera, eyes rolling back in his head and body convulsing maniacally, is one of the abiding memories of the World Cup.

After a win in the next game against Nigeria, Maradona left the field with a nurse escorting him to the drug-testing facility. That was how one of the World Cup's most talented and most flawed stars left the field for the last time.

He tested positive, although not for cocaine – for ephedrine, which he claimed had been in a power drink, the label of which he had not read. FIFA did not buy the excuse and sent him home. Argentina crashed out in the second round against Romania. Maradona was deemed a disgrace. He would play just 31 more games of football.

61

WORLD CUP LEGENDS

○ Maradona raises his hands to the heavens from a box at the Saint Petersburg Stadium prior to Argentina's Group D clash with Nigeria during the 2018 World Cup

For a footballing genius forever haunted by demons and weighed down by a burden of expectation no mortal could shoulder forever, it was a fittingly tragic end to a playing career that transcended what had previously been thought possible.

With his boots finally hung up, and a brief but unsuccessful first spell in management behind him, Maradona remained in the grip of the one constant in his life: cocaine. In 2000 he collapsed in Uruguay as a result of hypertension and an irregular heartbeat caused by his addiction. Narrowly avoiding death, Maradona would move to Cuba in 2002 in a bid to finally kick the habit that was destroying him. Yet despite eventually freeing himself of drugs, health problems were never far away. Neither was the spotlight.

In 2005 Maradona hosted the first episode of a talk show titled *The Night of the No. 10*, interviewing his long-time friend and rival Pelé. High-profile figures including Fidel Castro and Mike Tyson would follow, each playing second fiddle to Argentina's favourite son, who inevitably proved to be a ratings sensation. But despite his success in the world of media, the pull of Maradona's one true love proved irresistible, and in 2008 he returned to management as head coach of the Argentina national team (see boxout on page 59).

Following a mixed World Cup campaign in South Africa in 2010 that had initially promised much but ended in a 4-0 hammering at the hands of a rampant Germany, Maradona found himself cast out after the Argentinian Football Association reneged on the offer of a contract extension.

Spells managing five different clubs in the UAE, Argentina and Mexico followed, but the incredible success Maradona enjoyed as a player never transferred to the dugout. In 2019 he took charge of Gimnasia de La Plata, a team located in Buenos Aires Province. It would prove to be his last.

On 25 November 2020, Diego Armando Maradona, the rebellious magician who had lit up the world with a ball at his feet, died at the age of just 60 in his home in the Argentine capital, a heart attack robbing him of life and the world of an icon.

○ Maradona bamboozles the Belgium defence during the 1982 World Cup, at which he scored twice

DIEGO MARADONA

Napoli fans mourn the passing of a man they hailed as a god

"SPELLS MANAGING FIVE CLUBS FOLLOWED, BUT THE SUCCESS HE ENJOYED AS A PLAYER NEVER TRANSFERRED TO THE DUGOUT"

Tributes poured in from every corner of the footballing community and beyond for a man many consider to have been the greatest player to ever grace a pitch. Among those to pay their respects was Pelé. "I have lost a dear friend, and the world has lost a legend. One day, I hope we will play football together in the sky."

It is often the fate of those who change the world to be taken before their time, and Maradona, the rambunctious pioneer who escaped the slum to conquer the world, had seemed exhausted by life for some time. And yet he always had a ready smile for everyone he met, be they an awed fan or a fellow professional. For he was, above all else, a man of the people. His people. After all, the most beautiful thing about Maradona, aside from his god-like ability, was that he wore his flaws with pride. No one has ever so perfectly illustrated what it is to be without equal and yet simultaneously just like everyone else. It is this trait, above all else, that makes the boy from Buenos Aires immortal.

REMEMBERING DIEGO

Whether you loved him or loathed him, one thing you could never do was ignore Diego Armando Maradona.
There are many things you can say about El Diego, but his ability with a football at his feet will always be the most important. He was the greatest player of his era and arguably the best player of any era.

He lit up the 1980s with his breathtaking skill and ability and reached unbelievable highs on an international level with Argentina and at club level first with Barcelona and then at Napoli.

He single-handedly drove Argentina to World Cup glory in Mexico in 1986, and if there were ever to be a 90 minutes that defined Maradona's career it would be the quarter-final at the Azteca Stadium against the old enemy of England.

In between the 51st and 55th minute Maradona showed the two sides of his game and personality, firstly when he made up for the height advantage England goalkeeper Peter Shilton had over him by punching the ball into the net before running off to celebrate as if he had scored with his head – a goal he later called 'the Hand of God'.

Then minutes later he received the ball in his own half from Hector Enrique and proceeded to go on a 60-yard run past Peter Beardsley, Peter Reid, Terry Butcher (twice) and Terry Fenwick before slotting the ball past Shilton in what is regarded as the greatest individual goal ever scored. Two goals remembered for very different reasons.

Maradona again scored twice in the semi-final win over Belgium before going on to lift the World Cup after Argentina beat West Germany 3-2 in the final.

If what he did with Argentina made him a football great, then his achievements with Napoli made him immortal.

He guided the unfancied Neapolitan side to two Scudettos and a UEFA Cup during the late 80s and early 90s – a feat that has never been matched.

Yes, his career, and life, were blighted by cocaine, cheating and craziness, and yes, Pelé may have scored more goals and Lionel Messi won more trophies, but when you saw Diego Maradona with the ball at his feet then nothing else mattered. He was a genius.

James Andrew
Editor, FourFourTwo

WORLD CUP LEGENDS

MANAGING GREAT EXPECTATIONS:
10 LEGENDARY WORLD CUP COACHES

There have been 20 World Cup-winning managers, but which of those stand out the most?

Coaching an international football team is rather different to managing a club side. For starters, those at the helm are unable to plug any gaps in their squad by splashing the cash. There is also far less time to iron out problems on the training pitch or in regular fixtures.

Indeed, with international management, there is a greater reliance on organisation and trust. It's important to manage egos and plan for the long term while bearing in mind that any disappointments can linger for months between matches. At the same time, coaches have the weight of expectation of their entire country on their shoulders. No wonder such jobs are widely seen as the toughest in football.

Yet, if carried out with success, they can lead to great prestige. Winning the English First Division title with Ipswich Town, just a year after gaining promotion from the second tier, was a tremendous achievement, for instance. Yet manager Alf Ramsey is more fondly remembered for winning the World Cup with England in 1966.

At the same time, the very best managers in the club game can have the shine taken off them at international level, no matter how fleetingly. Alex Ferguson managed Scotland to the 1986 World Cup following the death of Jock Stein, but his team ended up bottom of Group E with defeats against Denmark and West Germany, and a draw against Uruguay. Nobody said it was easy.

It's with this in mind that we look at the ten most legendary coaches in World Cup history, and it wasn't easy boiling them down. Sepp Herberger, for instance, masterminded West Germany's World Cup win in 1954, with his side defeating the runaway favourites Hungary 3-2. Juan López Fontana won the cup for Uruguay on Brazilian soil.

But what we have here are ten coaches who have made a huge impression on the tournament for the numerous reasons that we go on to explain. Ever since Alberto Suppici won the inaugural competition in 1930 with Uruguay, the eyes of the world have been upon men such as these, with only one of our top ten coaches now looked upon more with disdain than the respect that he undoubtedly deserves.

That, however, is football, and the measure of expectation. Just as every England manager feels duty-bound to bring the World Cup back to the country that invented football, so past triumphs and the club achievements of the world's greatest players add an extra layer of burden for the managers. It's a funny old game, after all.

TOP WORLD CUP COACHES

VITTORIO POZZO
THE ONLY COACH TO WIN TWICE

Although Vittorio Pozzo managed Italy for 19 years over three spells between 1912 and 1948, the man known as 'Il Vecchio Maestro' – 'the Old Master' – ensured his legendary status in the mid-to-late 1930s.

Having created the Metodo tactical formation – a 2-3-2-3, dubbed the W-W because of the shape it formed on the pitch – he led the Azzuri to World Cup victory twice, in 1934 and 1938. In doing so he became the first and only manager to lift the trophy twice.

As if to show just how great he was as a manager, he supplemented that by steering his team to Olympic gold in Berlin in 1936 – a victory that supporters of Italian dictator Benito Mussolini claimed was vindication of the fascist system's superiority.

But Pozzo had actually fallen in love with football in socialist-leaning Manchester, where he had studied at the turn of the 20th century. He was inspired by Manchester United's centre-half Charlie Roberts, who he regarded as the best player in the world.

Indeed, it is understood that Roberts influenced the style that Pozzo went on to adopt. He placed a greater reliance on the inside forwards rather than the centre-half, and this unleashed Internazionale's Giuseppe Meazza and Juventus's Giovanni Ferrari, both of whom – along with Eraldo Monzeglio – are the only Italians to have won two World Cups. Although Italy did not compete in the first World Cup in 1930, his team lifted the Central European International Cup that year.

He also controversially brought South American-born Italian nationals into the team, pointing to their role in the Italian army as justification. At the 1934 World Cup in Italy, they beat the USA 7-1 in the first round, overcame Spain 1-0 in a quarter-final replay and saw off Austria in the semi-final, beating Czechoslovakia 2-1 after extra time in the final.

Thanks to his dedication and determination, however, Pozzo sought to improve the team for 1938 in France, building it around Meazza and Ferrari. They beat Norway 2-1 in their opening match, before knocking out the hosts in the quarter-final 3-1. They then defeated Brazil in the semis and put four past Hungary in the final, conceding two to become victors once again.

WORLD CUP LEGENDS

FRANZ BECKENBAUER
THE MAN THEY CALL 'DER KAISER'

As a player, Franz Beckenbauer captained West Germany to World Cup glory in 1974. He also led Bayern Munich to three European Cups and earned himself the nickname 'Der Kaiser' – 'The Emperor'. His stock kept rising after he stopped playing.

Appointed the team supervisor of West Germany in 1984 because he lacked a coaching qualification, he nevertheless took his unfancied team to the World Cup final in 1986. And while they ended up on the losing side against a Diego Maradona-inspired Argentina (beaten 3-2 in front of 114,600 people in the Estadio Azteca, Mexico City), the experience proved invaluable for the next tournament.

After coming a comfortable second in the qualifiers, they found themselves at Italia '90, topping Group D before beating the Netherlands, Czechoslovakia and England to reach the final. Once again their opponents were Argentina, but this time they had Jurgen Klinsmann, Lothar Matthäus and Rudi Völler.

Beckenbauer, who had also shown his natural leadership qualities in 1974 and stopped that team from falling apart, used his immense tactical insight and tight, organised footballing discipline to thwart their opponents, winning 1-0. In doing so, he became only the second man after Mário Zagallo of Brazil to win the World Cup both as a player and manager.

In 1990, assistant Berti Vogts said Beckenbauer had only been a "proper coach" for two years, but it didn't prevent him winning the World Cup

Vicente del Bosque took Spain to the 2010 and 2014 World Cups

VICENTE DEL BOSQUE
A GENTLE WINNER

By the time Vicente del Bosque took the reins of Spain in 2008, the nation's football team had won the UEFA European Championship with a team that included Andrés Iniesta, Xavi Hernández, Sergio Ramos and David Silva. Their style and structure was already ingrained, but del Bosque was not afraid of making changes in a bid to evolve the team.

Spain were the favourites to win the tournament, yet they lost their opening match against Switzerland. Rather than change the game plan, del Bosque stood firm and put faith in his players, dealing with the situation with a trademark calmness. By building the team around Sergio Busquets and Xabi Alonso and retaining the short passing and movement of the tiki-taka style of play, they progressed to the final, beating England, Argentina and Germany on the way.

Del Bosque then looked at the devastating potential of the Netherlands and sought to make good use of Jesus Navas' speed on the right wing. The game was forced into extra time, but Iniesta scored in the 116th minute to hand victory to Spain. He then led the team to further European Championship glory two years later.

TOP WORLD CUP COACHES

CARLOS BILARDO
DOC WITH A CURE FOR FAILURE

While it's fair to say that the 1986 World Cup will be forever associated with Diego Maradona, Argentina's victory was actually down to the tactics of the coach, Carlos Bilardo. He successfully introduced the 3-5-2 formation – the first time it had been used in a major tournament – and in doing so promoted the virtues of a pragmatic game played to win rather than entertain.

Bilardo was an unusual coach, not least because he was also a trained gynaecologist. Obsessed with tactics and deeply superstitious, he followed his playing career with management spells at Estudiantes, Deportivo Cali and San Lorenzo. He coached the Colombian national team before being appointed Argentina's coach in 1983, and arrived with a reputation for anti-football.

But he was also a grafter, meticulously preparing for games. He nurtured Maradona, appointing him captain, then switched from 4-4-2 to 3-5-2 soon after the 1986 World Cup got underway. This freed Maradona and allowed Jorge Burruchaga and Jorge Valdano to attack, while forcing the rest of the team to remain solid and well-practised.

It wasn't pretty, but it worked. Argentina dispatched England in the quarters, beat Belgium and won 3-2 against West Germany.

○ Even though Bilardo won the World Cup in 1986, some called for him to resign over his method of play

HELMUT SCHÖN
VETERAN OF FOUR WORLD CUPS

Helmut Schön was born in Dresden in 1915, a city that found itself part of Soviet-occupied East Germany after the World War II. Political interference prompted him to flee to the West in 1950, and it was there that he became a true legend.

Schön was appointed manager of West Germany in November 1964. It was Schön's team that faced England in the World Cup final of 1966, forcing the game into extra time, only to suffer the blow of a double-strike by Geoff Hurst to lose 4-2 at Wembley Stadium.

He exacted revenge in the World Cup quarter-final of 1970. Defeat to Italy in the semis, however, saw West Germany console themselves with a third-place finish. Yet in 1972, West Germany became European champions.

There was a sense that Schön would eventually crack the World Cup, and so it came in 1974 with West Germany hosting. Building the team around captain Beckenbauer, they topped the table in the second round and faced the Netherlands in the final, running out 2-1 winners.

He then took West Germany to the final of the European Championship two years later. Yet they were beaten by Czechoslovakia on penalties and, while they qualified as champions for the 1978 World Cup, they lost out in the quarters. It didn't stop him being Germany's most successful national coach.

○ Schön won 16 of his 25 World Cup matches, drawing five and losing just four

WORLD CUP LEGENDS

"THE MOVE FROM A HIGHLY ORGANISED DEFENCE TO SOMETHING APPROACHING TOTAL FOOTBALL WAS A SUCCESS"

○ Italy's 1986 campaign was not as successful as 1982, but Bearzot left his job, having coached Italy for a record 104 games

TOP WORLD CUP COACHES

ENZO BEARZOT
THE MAN WHO BROKE ITALY'S 44-YEAR DROUGHT

Although Enzo Bearzot only had a single cap for Italy as a player, he was determined to make his mark as a manager when he became the joint head coach of his country alongside Fulvio Bernardini in 1975. He soon took over entirely and led the team to three World Cups in 1978, 1982 and 1986, transforming the side from one that prioritised cynical and brutal defending to a group of players that flourished in attack.

In his first tournament, Italy came a respectable fourth and Bearzot, who had been an assistant to Ferruccio Valcareggi four years earlier, was praised for his team's flexible and exciting play. He took the same sense of adventure to the 1982 tournament, although three poorly played draws in Group 1 drew criticism from supporters and saw him impose a media blackout.

The 'silenzio stampa', however, turned out to be a masterstroke. By shielding his players from the press, he worked purely on encouraging the team. They began to play well, beating Argentina and Brazil, knocking out Poland in the semis and seeing off West Germany 3-1 in the final – a first World Cup win since 1938. The move from a highly organised defence to something approaching total football was deemed a success, as was his decision to recall Paolo Rossi after a two-year ban for match fixing. Rossi repaid him with a top-scoring six goals.

○ Mário Zagallo adopted a loose starting XI in 1970 that made use of Brazil's finest players

MÁRIO ZAGALLO
THE EVER-PRESENT BRAZILIAN

Mário Zagallo owned the number 10 shirt that Pelé wore in the first half of the 1970 World Cup final. He put it up for auction in 2007, but it always held a special memory for him, not least because 1970 was the tournament in which Brazil trod an unbeaten path to a 4-1 victory against Italy. While Zagallo had only been appointed three months earlier, he had just overseen a team that, arguably, was the best to ever grace a World Cup pitch.

But then Zagallo was no stranger to the tournament. He had won the World Cup as a player in 1958 and 1962, which meant, 1966 aside, he'd had a phenomenal run. For 1970, he had switched attacking midfielder Rivellino to the left wing, allowing midfielder Gérson a place and he restored goalkeeper Félix Miélli Venerando. It showed that his tactics were astute, and that his attention to detail was equally acute.

Zagallo still had his clipboard in his hand when he was celebrating Brazil's victory. But what is perhaps just as remarkable is that he led Brazil in more World Cups. A lacklustre 1974 saw the team finish in fourth place (he quit shortly after), while in 1998 in France, he took them all the way to the final, where the hosts beat them 3-0. He was also made caretaker of Brazil in 2002 and coordinator between 2003 and 2006.

WORLD CUP LEGENDS

VICENTE FEOLA
THE CONTROVERSIAL WINNER

It is perhaps unfair that many Brazilians view Vicente Feola with a tinge of bitterness, focusing less on their country's first World Cup title in 1958 and more on their disastrous performance in 1966. For while he did chalk up just one victory in England (a 2-0 win against Bulgaria), he had the foresight of introducing Pelé – then aged just 17 – in 1958. He scored against Wales in the quarters, put three past France in the semis and two past Sweden in the final. Winning that latter game 5-2 showed how strong Brazil were.

Even so, the stockily built Feola had a reputation for being a little too laid back, and stories emerged of him sleeping on the bench and letting senior players take too much control. He also had a large coaching team consisting of a doctor, fitness coach, team supervisor, psychologist and even a dentist – a novelty at the time. Yet players have since affirmed that Feola was indeed making the decisions, and that he got them enjoying an expansive game. His groundwork paved the way for a second success in 1962, although he was too ill to oversee that one himself.

○ Feola kickstarted Brazil's phenomenal success of five World Cup victories back in 1958

○ Joachim Löw's Germany entered the 2018 World Cup as defending champions after winning all ten of their qualifying matches en route to the tournament

JOACHIM LÖW
HIS WINNING TEAM HUMBLED BRAZIL ON HOME SOIL

Having made his way into coaching when he broke his shin bone as a player aged 22, Joachim Löw eventually became Germany's manager in 2006, giving him the chance of putting a lifetime of studying the game into good effect at the highest of levels.

Prior to that, Löw had short spells at clubs such as VfB Stuttgart, Fenerbahçe and Tirol Innsbruck. But his initial partnership as assistant coach to Jürgen Klinsmann had seen Germany come third at the 2006 World Cup. Löw repeated that effort in 2010 before finally bagging Germany's fourth World Cup in 2014, beating Argentina 1-0 in the final after inflicting Brazil's worst World Cup defeat (7-1) in the semis before their home crowd, highlighting their confidence and aggression.

His side followed up their triumph in Brazil by lifting the FIFA Confederations Cup for the first time in 2017, having reached the semi-finals of the European Championship the year before. However, 2018 certainly didn't go to plan, with Germany crashing out in the group stages following defeats to Mexico and South Korea. They then endured an equally uninspiring EURO 2020, beaten 2-0 in the Round of 16 by England. Löw stepped down after the tournament, perhaps regretting that he had not done so while on a high.

TOP WORLD CUP COACHES

> Ramsey's decision to play a tight, direct midfield in a 4-4-2 formation ensured England were dubbed the wingless wonders

ALF RAMSEY
THE MANAGER WHO BROUGHT FOOTBALL HOME

When Alf Ramsey was appointed manager of England on the back of enormous success with Ipswich Town - a team he led from the Third Division to champions of the First Division in the space of seven whirlwind years - he made a bold declaration: "We will win the World Cup."

It was a statement that fans couldn't quite believe that day in October 1962. But it was clear that he wanted to do things his own way. His predecessor, Walter Winterbottom, did not have control over team selections, but that was not Ramsey's style. Indeed, he named Bobby Moore as captain even though the player was just 22 years and 47 days old.

Ramsey didn't start well. His first match was a preliminary round qualifier for the European Nations Cup on 27 February 1963, which England lost 5-2. But England had qualified for the World Cup in 1966 as hosts and Ramsey was keen to capitalise on that home advantage, even though on paper it was clear England were not the best team in the tournament.

He sought to calm his players, even allowing them to watch *Those Magnificent Men In Their Flying Machines* at a local cinema the day before the first game. He treated the side like a club team, and sought to make it as close-knit as possible. This ensured the whole was greater than the sum of its parts and, despite a 0-0 draw with Uruguay, England went all the way.

In doing so, Ramsey proved he was unafraid of making difficult decisions. Striker Jimmy Greaves was injured in the group stage, for instance, allowing Geoff Hurst to take his place in the quarter-final. When Greaves recovered and the press pondered whether he would play in the final, Ramsey stuck with Hurst. It paid off, as Hurst scored a hat-trick to sink West Germany 4-2.

Unfortunately, the momentum did not continue. Ramsey took England to third place in the UEFA European Championship in 1968, but his teams suffered quarter-final defeats at the 1970 World Cup and 1972 Euros. He also failed to qualify for the 1974 World Cup. Yet that 1966 victory for England - which was, in many ways, won against the odds despite Ramsey's optimism - has been enough to make him a true legend for his country. His tactical approach, strictness and demands for high performance won out, and the victory will always be remembered.

WORLD CUP LEGENDS

ZINEDINE ZIDANE:
A TALE OF TWO FINALS

Zidane went from hero to zero between 1998 and 2006, highlighting a supreme talent mixed with a fiery temperament

It was 18 June 1998, and France were playing Saudi Arabia in their second game of the first round of the World Cup. They were comfortably 2-0 up thanks to goals by Thierry Henry and David Trezeguet, and Zinedine Zidane was in typically fine form. He was enjoying his second ever World Cup tournament match following the game against South Africa six days before. On that occasion, he received a yellow card in the 75th minute for pulling at Quinton Fortune. This time, however, he would literally see red.

In the 71st minute, Zidane was tackled by the Saudi defender Fuad Amin, who fell to the floor in a tangle of legs. Rather than walk away, Zidane brought his foot down hard on his opponent's body, and the referee, Arturo Brizio Carter, had no hesitation in reaching for his pocket. It was only good fortune for Zidane that France continued to power forward with ten men and bag two more goals to make it 4-0.

As subsequent footage shows, a frustrated Zidane rubbed his face in contemplation as he sat alone in the dressing room. He knew what could so easily have happened following that moment of madness. But had he learned his lesson? France certainly hoped so.

During those first two games, Zidane had displayed the sublime skills that were to become his trademark. He had spun 180 degrees out of a challenge against Saudi Arabia, for instance, to flick a pass to Bixente Lizarazu that ended at the feet of Henry for the opener. It had also been his corner that allowed Christophe Dugarry to open France's account against South Africa. But then it was always abundantly clear that Zidane was an exceptional talent playing in a superb French team. Yet that temper. That temper!

To understand where it may have come from, it's worth delving into Zidane's past.

ZINEDINE ZIDANE

○ Zidane heads France into the lead against Brazil during the 1998 World Cup final

Born in Marseille, France, on 23 June 1972 to parents of Algerian descent, Zidane had spent much of his youth kicking a ball around the tower blocks of the bleak modernist council estate in Marseille's tough La Castellane neighbourhood, where many first and second-generation immigrants resided to form a close-knit, life-affirming community.

He'd ended up joining a local football club called US Saint-Henri at the age of ten years old before signing for SO Septèmes-les-Vallons a year later. Duly selected to attend a footballing institute run by the French Football Federation, he was then spotted by AS Cannes in 1986, turning professional three years later. He remained with the club until 1992, when he joined Bordeaux - a great move that saw them win the Intertoto Cup in 1995, but finish runners-up against Bayern Munich in the 1996 UEFA Cup Final, losing 5-1 over two legs.

By then, however, Zidane had already decided to move to Juventus, where he went on to help the team win two league titles, a Supercoppa Italiana, a UEFA Super Cup and an Intercontinental Cup. All of that prepared him well for the 1998 World Cup, and he had clearly shown what he could do. There were sharp glimpses of his internal vision, precise control and immense drive. He also showed an ability to run forward with extraordinary pace, and he was already well on his way to becoming the most complete footballer of his generation, even at that early stage.

Indeed, pundits and fans were constantly amazed that he could find space out of nothing and inspire confidence in those around him simply by being there. They were mesmerised by his mastering of the Marseille Turn, a specialised dribbling skill also employed by Maradona that would see him drag his strong foot back, spin his body

WORLD CUP LEGENDS

THE GOLDEN BALL

Prior to the 2006 World Cup final in Berlin, Zinedine Zidane was awarded the prestigious Golden Ball, which is handed out to the best player of the tournament. The then-34 year old had topped a poll of journalists covering the World Cup that summer and, having taken their pick from a list of players collated by the FIFA technical committee, the media gave Zidane 2,012 points – a tally which just edged him ahead of Fabio Cannavaro of Italy, who received 1,977 points. It was way more than the 715 points given to Andrea Pirlo, also of Italy.

What is most likely to have swung it for Zidane – who was not only lacklustre in the opening two group matches, but sent off in the final – were his blistering performances against Spain, Brazil and Portugal in the knock-out rounds. He'd been named man of the match against Brazil, during which he assisted Thierry Henry's deciding goal. Meanwhile, his penalty against Portugal had put France into the final. For Zidane, who was retiring at the end of the tournament, winning this prestigious accolade was an opportunity for glory amid controversy and disappointment.

---

and then drag his weaker foot backwards, befuddling opponents.

So to have Zidane out for the next two games in 1998 courtesy of that red card took some of the wind out of France's sails. They may well have triumphed over Denmark and Paraguay without him (they beat Denmark 2-1 and Paraguay 1-0) but, in that latter game at least, they embarrassingly flapped and floundered at times. France needed a sudden death goal against Paraguay courtesy of Laurent Blanc to send them into the quarters. This, however, allowed Zidane to return to the tournament and seize his chance.

Perhaps eager not to put another foot wrong, he was actually relatively subdued in the subsequent stalemate quarter-final against Italy, even though he scored the first penalty in the shootout to help France through 4-3. He wasn't his true pioneering self against Croatia in the semis either but, again, France's overall strength saw them through with a 2-1 win. The victory put France into the final against Brazil, and there was no doubt that France needed Zidane to be at his best. All he needed to do was keep his fiery temperament under control, and everyone knew he would be hugely effective.

So it came: 12 July 1998. The French supporters were heaping much pressure on Zidane's shoulders, their usual enthusiastic shouts of "Zidane" bouncing off the roof of the magnificent Stade de France. By this stage, 'Zizoumania' – as the press called it in reference to Zidane's nickname, Zizou – was in full flow. The French supporters were hopeful that the team could finally lift the trophy for the first time following the disappointments of 1958, 1982 and 1986, when the country failed to get past the semis.

To get this far had not been without effort and sacrifice. To keep the team focused, they had been staying in hotels far away from their families and this had led them to think only of their single objective: to lift the golden trophy in Paris and become champions of the world. Nerves had begun to jangle as the team stood before the 75,000-strong crowd, but when the whistle blew, Les Bleus showed their intent. Almost immediately, Zidane was displaying his intricate passing and incandescent skills, his confidence raised and a sense of victory already apparent.

If there was any hint that the level of passionate support had weighed heavy on the team and that the demands on the players were high, the players looked determined not to show it. Some pundits had suggested that the immense expectation in France is what had caused Zidane to explode with such force during that game against the Saudis.

One thing's for sure, however: Zidane's temperament improved after he returned, and it was evident in this match. It was his chance to stand alongside the greats of the World Cup, from Pelé to Platini, Cruyff to Maradona – not that Zidane, a man of uncharacteristic humility, would have welcomed the comparisons in reality

Indeed, Zidane was always aware of his roots and, having worked hard, any victory would be entirely earned. He just had to keep the temper and the street-toughness he learned in the 'ghetto' under strict control. The good news was that he was seemingly more relaxed than he had been at the start of the tournament, when his teammates noticed he was more stretched and demanding.

Easing matters for Zidane was the fact that he wasn't actually the talking point as the game got underway; Brazil's Ronaldo was. About 70 minutes before the kick-off, the footballing press had become rather giddy when they noticed that the man widely considered to be the greatest player at the tournament was not on the team sheet. Journalists spent 40 minutes looking for answers, only to be handed a replacement sheet with Ronaldo in place of Edmundo. An odd state of affairs, it only later became apparent that the striker had suffered a terrible fit while sleeping earlier in the day. Some who witnessed it thought he was dying.

The episode was put down to pressure, which had been too much for the 21 year old. Zidane would have understood. But just as Ronaldo appeared lost and a mere shadow of the player everyone knew him to be, so Zidane put on a masterclass. It therefore became an intriguing final between a country that had won the World Cup four times – the last just four years earlier in 1994 – and a team that seemed to embody the world. That's because France was made up of players with roots in Africa, South America, the Caribbean, Armenia and the Basque country. It was so

"ZIDANE WAS DISPLAYING HIS INTRICATE PASSING AND INCANDESCENT SKILLS, A SENSE OF VICTORY ALREADY APPARENT"

ZINEDINE ZIDANE

Zidane in action during the 1998 World Cup final between Brazil and France. France would defeat Brazil 3-0

○ Zidane takes on Brazilian captain Dunga in the 1998 World Cup final

ZINEDINE ZIDANE

diverse that Jean-Marie Le Pen, leader of the far-right Front National party, called them "unworthy" to represent France – a disgraceful label and slur against the side that is only likely to have spurred them on further.

And so it was that Zidane had his moment, making entertaining runs that culminated in him scoring two first-half goals: one in the 27th minute when he headed a corner from Emmanuel Petit past goalkeeper Cláudio Taffarel and the other on 45, again from a corner. As the second half got underway, it was becoming ever more clear that Zidane would be man of the match, but France didn't make it easy for themselves.

Marcel Desailly, who was at the heart of the French defence, got a yellow card in the 48th minute and another in the 68th, which led to him being sent off. Down to ten men, it was ripe for a Brazilian comeback but France – and Zidane – remained strong, particularly in their defensive performance and their collective decision to continue to push forward.

Then, in the 90th minute, Emmanuel Petit got on the end of a pass from Patrick Vieira and the game was over. France had won 3-0 and Zidane had become a national hero, his face later projected onto the Arc de Triomphe, complete with the phrase "Zizou on t'aime" ("Zizou, we love you"). In achieving such an upset against the previous tournament's champions, Zidane – who was indeed man of the match – had helped turn France on to the delights of international football after years of apathy. The celebrations continued on the Champs-Élysées long into the night.

Zidane's stock had risen hugely. The following season, he won the Intertoto Cup with Juventus and France picked up the European Championship in 2000. A year later, Zidane signed a four-year deal with Real Madrid worth a then-record £46 million. He was 29 years old, and his immediate goal was to steer the club to a ninth European Cup. Zidane-mania was felt on the streets of Madrid and he picked up the Supercopa de España almost immediately.

By the end of that season, he'd added the Champions League, but internationally, things were less rosy. A thigh injury stopped him from playing in France's opening games in the 2002 World Cup and by the time he came back, in the third group match, it was largely too late and he couldn't prevent his country from being eliminated. Still, back with Madrid, he ended up winning La Liga in the 2002-03

WHAT DID MATERAZZI SAY?

When Zinedine Zidane was sent off in the final of the 2006 World Cup, it was clear that the Italian defender Marco Materazzi had said something to him. Quite what, however, was the subject of speculation that was only properly cleared up a year later when Materazzi revealed the actual words.

It appears Zidane had reacted to having his shirt pulled by Materazzi and told him: "If you want my shirt I will give it to you afterwards." Materazzi revealed to the magazine *TV Sorrisi e Canzoni* that he then replied to the French star: "I prefer the whore that is your sister." This caused Zidane to retaliate.

But does Zidane regret it? Maybe. He admitted to the French sports television programme *Téléfoot* in 2017 that he was ashamed of what happened that day. "I am not proud of this gesture – for all these young people, all these coaches, all these volunteers who make football a different thing," he told them.

Yet, when asked in 2010 if he would say sorry to Materazzi, he was unequivocal. "I'd rather die," he answered, explaining: "If I say 'sorry', I would also be admitting that what he himself did was normal. And for me it was not normal."

WORLD CUP LEGENDS

Mexican referee Arturo Brizio Carter sends off Zidane for stamping on the Saudi captain Fuad Amin in 1998

season, while picking up the UEFA Super Cup, Intercontinental Cup and another Supercopa de España. It was some haul in such a small space of time, and Zidane soon found himself preparing for another World Cup.

Germany 2006 was set to be Zidane's last. He'd already announced that he would retire a year earlier, but he was persuaded to give his all for one more World Cup. Some saw him as France's great hope and not just in a footballing sense. Politically, it was hoped he could deflect attention from high unemployment and other such problems back home. To that degree, the pressure was upon

him yet again, although the external factors were now wider than football itself, and it could be argued that it was too much for him to take on.

In reality, very few people thought France could win the World Cup this time around, but Zidane vowed to himself to go out with a bang. It's just a shame that it wasn't quite the bang he would have hoped for, as history would bear out.

Just as in the 1998 World Cup, Zidane picked up a yellow card in his opening game against Switzerland, this time in the 72nd minute, which was three short of the previous

occasion. France drew 0-0 and went on to play South Korea, hoping to turn things around. Instead, they drew 1-1 and Zidane got yet another caution in the 85th minute. It meant he missed the 2-0 victory over Togo that saw France scrape through to the knockout stage, but in a bid to get the players motivated, he told them: "We live together, we will die together". Things began to get better after that.

France thumped three past Spain to win 3-1 in the Round of 16, with Zidane getting a yellow card in the 91st minute before scoring 60 seconds later. Supporters were overjoyed

ZINEDINE ZIDANE

ZIDANE FACTS & FIGURES

3 GOALS SCORED IN WORLD CUP FINAL MATCHES

1 GAMES PLAYED AT 2002 WORLD CUP

108 OVERALL NUMBER OF APPEARANCES FOR FRANCE

2 NUMBER OF RED CARDS RECEIVED IN WORLD CUP MATCHES

12 MATCHES PLAYED IN WORLD CUPS

2 NUMBER OF APPEARANCES IN THE FIFA ALL-STAR TEAM (1998, 2006)

that the Frenchman seemed to have found his rhythm and he was cajoling his teammates to victory, conjuring images of 1998. Zidane did the same against Brazil in the quarter-finals, which France won 1-0, and his penalty in the 33rd minute of the semi-final against Portugal put his country through to the final.

And so it was that on 9 July 2006, Zidane would play his last game for France before a crowd of 69,000 at the Olympiastadion in Berlin against Italy. Zidane got a penalty in the seventh minute but Materazzi equalised. The game went into extra time and then Zidane seemingly exploded, with ten minutes to go before the whistle blew for penalties. He well and truly lost his head.

After nearly heading France to victory only to see Italy's goalkeeper Gianluigi Buffon take hold, he got involved in an altercation with Materazzi. It had originally been thought that Materazzi had insulted Zidane's mother, but the defender later admitted it was his sister. Either way, it riled Zidane, who initially walked past the player before deciding to turn and walk back to him. With his head down, he butted Materazzi in the chest, prompting him to fall theatrically to the floor. Zidane got a red card and France lost the game on penalties.

Even today, it's a moment that cannot be forgotten – an inglorious ending to an iconic playing career. Pundits believed it may have caused France to lose what would have been their second World Cup title, and Zidane has never argued that it was undeserved. In fact, he has since said his sending off was "a very good thing" because he could not have lived with France becoming world champions if he had stayed on the pitch after what he'd done. It was a noble response from a stunning, albeit flawed player whose passion for the game could never be questioned. But how different the story could have been.

79

WORLD CUP LEGENDS

TOTAL FOOTBALL AND THE BIRTH OF THE MODERN GAME

Although they came up short, the 1974 Netherlands side is remembered as one of the very best

Which World Cup side is the greatest of them all?

Clearly, a string of wins against the world's best teams is a prerequisite for any candidate, as is an exciting, aesthetically pleasing style of football. The same goes for a healthy smattering of star names, and a classic kit always helps.

What about sides who never actually won the World Cup? Can they be considered too? Devotees of the Netherlands side of the 1974 World Cup would likely say so.

In coach Rinus Michels and captain Johan Cruyff the Oranje of the 1970s were served by two giants of world football. The team will also be remembered for their swaggering, often breathtaking, performances in West Germany over the course of the summer of 1974. They won all but one of six matches in the first two group stages, scoring 14 times and conceding just once.

Argentina, a technically gifted side who went on to win the World Cup four years later, were swatted aside 4-0 in a ruthless display.

Then it was the turn of Brazil, winners of three of the previous four tournaments. Unable to deal with the constant swarm of orange jerseys, the Seleção could count themselves lucky not to have been beaten by a greater margin than 2-0.

Results aside, what made the 1974 Netherlands team exceptional was a set of bold, new tactics. The origins of Total Football, or totaalvoetbal in Dutch, can be traced as far back as Matthias Sindelar's Austrian national team of the 1930s, through River Plate's La Máquina a decade later, and Ferenc Puskás's Hungary of the 1950s. It really took off under Michels at Ajax from 1965 onwards, though.

Given that Total Football is most commonly associated with the free-scoring Ajax and Dutch national sides of the 1970s, as well as Barcelona from the late 1980s onwards, its underlying premise is surprisingly a defensive one. That is, if the opponent does not have the ball, he cannot score. The idea is to make the pitch as small as possible when out of possession. This is done by pushing the defensive line up the pitch to set an aggressive offside trap, while your own attackers press the opponent deep in his own half.

For the Dutch team, this meant quick transitions from a 4-3-3 to a 3-4-3, with the sweeper pushing into midfield, as the situation dictated. As such, the system required players to become adept at playing in more than just one position – a largely alien concept in the 1970s.

Michels' Ajax had used Total Football to devastating effect in the early 1970s, winning four Eredivisie titles, three KNVB Cups and a European Cup, before he exported it to Barcelona. But before the age of satellite TV and online football streaming, it had been witnessed by very few outside Amsterdam and Catalonia.

The watching world was stunned by what the Netherlands were doing, as the World Cup was beamed across the world. Their game differed from that of their opponents so

TOTAL FOOTBALL

Johan Cruyff under pressure from a West German defender in the 1974 World Cup final

WORLD CUP LEGENDS

radically, they may as well have been playing an entirely new sport.

Footage from the tournament - available at the click of a button these days - is quite a sight. In match after match, gangs of orange shirts streamed across the pitch in what seemed to be counter-intuitive patterns.

Instead of closing down passing lanes, Michels' men chased after individual opponents, while six or more defenders would sprint in unison towards the halfway line to leave dawdling opponents stranded offside.

While tactical change in football is largely evolutionary rather than revolutionary, it is not reductive to argue that the sport's history can be divided in two by the 1974 World Cup; football before Cruyff and after Cruyff, such has been Total Football's far-reaching and enduring impact. Its fingerprints can be found everywhere in the modern game.

"As a small boy," Arrigo Sacchi, the legendary Milan manager, once said, "I was in love with Honvéd, then Real Madrid, then Brazil, all the great sides. But it was Holland in the 1970s that really took my breath away. It was a mystery to me. The television was too small; I felt like I need to see the whole pitch fully to understand what they were doing and fully to appreciate it."

Today, tactical flexibility and off-the-ball movement are so prevalent that almost all top-level European club sides can be considered exponents of Total Football.

Leaving Ajax for Barcelona, as Michels had done, Cruyff's ideas later became enmeshed in the footballing DNA of what became the modern era's pre-eminent team. The tactical approach of the Spanish national sides that won three consecutive major tournaments can also be traced back to Total Football.

Pep Guardiola, the then-Barcelona manager, who had played under Cruyff, once remarked: "Cruyff built the cathedral. Our job is to maintain and renovate it."

If a team's greatness is at least partly measured by its wider impact on its sport, the 1974 Dutch team can be said to have played some of the most important football of the 20th century.

Of course, football is much more than Xs and Os on a blackboard. The legendary Oranje team was also touched by technical genius and scintillating link-up play between Cruyff and forwards Johnny Rep and Rob Rensenbrink.

Cute passes, often with the outside of the boot, were employed to great effect, while emboldened attackers introduced tricks and flicks to their game.

> "IT WAS HOLLAND IN THE 1970S THAT REALLY TOOK MY BREATH AWAY. IT WAS A MYSTERY TO ME" ARRIGO SACCHI

○ Like the 1974 team, the Dutch side of 1978 would also come up short in the World Cup final – this time against Argentina

TOTAL FOOTBALL

The Cruyff turn, in which a player shapes to pass before dragging the ball back behind his standing leg and wheeling away, was debuted during the Netherlands' match against Sweden in the 1974 World Cup. Within weeks, players across the world were attempting to imitate the now-famous technique.

The Dutch went into the final against a Franz Beckenbauer-led West Germany as hot favourites, despite playing in front of a partisan crowd in Munich's Olympiastadion. There was also an inevitable whiff of tension around the ground. It was just three decades removed from the Nazi invasion of the Netherlands, the event that has fuelled a decades-long rivalry between the two nations.

The away side made the best possible start; Johan Neeskens converted from the penalty spot after just two minutes following a rash challenge on Cruyff by Uli Hoeneß.

However, as the match wore on, the Germans began to grow into it. It soon became apparent that they had worked with a plan to neutralise the Dutch tactics. Right-back Berti Vogts was charged with dealing with the threat of Cruyff and marking the Netherlands' star players out of the game, while Beckenbauer, Hoeneß and Wolfgang Overath flooded the midfield and took charge of the game.

Paul Breitner levelled the scores from the spot midway through the first half, and Gerd Müller added a second on the stroke of half time. Stifled for the first time in the tournament, Michels' men failed to find another goal, and West Germany were crowned world champions.

They may not have lifted the trophy but the men in orange jerseys nevertheless remain one of the most important football teams ever assembled. Few would argue their status as the greatest team never to win the World Cup.

"Maybe we were the real winners in the end," Cruyff mused, teasingly in 2014, two years before his death. "I think the world remembers our team more."

THE ARCHITECT OF MODERN FOOTBALL

As almost every team in Europe's top leagues practises a form of Total Football, it's clear why it is considered the world's most successful philosophy.

Tiki-taka, an evolution of Total Football, underpinned the two pre-eminent sides of the modern era – Pep Guardiola's Barcelona and the Spanish team that won three major tournaments between 2008 and 2012.

It is no exaggeration to argue that Johan Cruyff, who played for Barcelona between 1973 and 1978, and then managed the side from 1988 until 1996, introduced many of the methods that helped it transform into the world's biggest club.

By 1990, Barça had won ten league titles and no European Cups in its history. Since then, it has collected 14 league titles and all five of its European Cups. Much of that is down to the club's enduring footballing philosophy, firmly rooted in Total Football, which remains in place even as managers come and go.

The system's success is also evident when one considers that managers with hugely differing styles – from Arsène Wenger to Ronald Koeman to Marcelo Bielsa – equally consider themselves disciples of Cruyff and Rinus Michels.

Of course, we mustn't forget there are a number of modern sides whose football more closely resembles Catenaccio, a defensive strategy characterised by nullifying an opponent's strengths, which was particularly popular in the 1960s.

But even José Mourinho and Diego Simeone, whose teams have been known to defend very deep at times, ask their players to be able to seamlessly switch positions and rapidly transition from defence to attack – hallmarks of Total Football.

WORLD CUP LEGENDS

TOP 10: GOALS

The World Cup has witnessed its share of stunning goals. Here we look back at some of the finest strikes ever seen on sport's biggest stage

CARLI LLOYD VS JAPAN, 2015

For sheer audacity, Lloyd's strike in the 2015 final is unrivalled. With the USA 3-0 up (Lloyd having scored a brace), the USA captain received the ball in the centre circle. Spotting Japan's Kaihori off her line, Lloyd sent an arching lob over the stricken keeper to make it 4-0.

CARLOS ALBERTO VS ITALY, 1970

In the 1970 final against Italy, Brazil were already 3-1 up when they dribbled out of their own half. Jairzinho found Pelé, a man determined to make a comeback after his 1966 injury, who laid the ball off for Carlos Alberto to thump home perhaps the greatest final goal ever.

ESTEBAN CAMBIASSO VS SERBIA AND MONTENEGRO, 2006

Argentina manager José Pékerman's philosophy was that consideration in possession, not frantic desperation, would always prevail. Never was that more obvious than when in a single minute, Argentina strung together 25 passes before Cambiasso scored from 12 yards out. The ultimate team goal.

EUSÉBIO VS BRAZIL, 1966

Some goals echo more for their significance and the players involved than their overall skill. Eusébio, known as the Black Panther, scored nine goals for Portugal at England '66. None resonated more than a half-volley, his second, to seal a 3-1 win over Brazil, knocking out the defending champions.

PELÉ VS SWEDEN, 1958

Brazil were behind after just four minutes of the final, but a Vavá double put them ahead before half time. Then Pelé produced a moment of magic, flicking the ball back over his defender's head to volley home from 15 yards and all but end the game as a contest.

TOP 10: GOALS

ROBIN VAN PERSIE VS SPAIN, 2014

⚽ **The opening game of Group B in 2014 was a re-run of the 2010 final, in which Andrés Iniesta had broken Dutch hearts.** The Netherlands got revenge in Brazil with a 5-1 win, but it was Robin van Persie's salmon-like leap and header from the edge of the box that lives long in the memory.

MICHAEL OWEN VS ARGENTINA, 1998

⚽ **The 1998 second-round clash between England and Argentina will be best remembered for Diego Simeone getting David Beckham sent off and David Batty's penalty miss.** But 18-year-old Michael Owen had already produced a memorable moment, beating José Chamot and Roberto Ayala in a run from the halfway line to score and give England a 2-1 lead.

SIPHIWE TSHABALALA VS MEXICO, 2010

⚽ **The 2010 World Cup was destined to be a special one – the very first in Africa.** And while the first half of the opening game of the tournament – South Africa vs Mexico – tested the eardrums with its vuvuzela volume, the second saw Siphiwe Tshabalala emphatically hammer home the first goal ever scored at an African World Cup. Bafana Bafana had announced themselves.

KYLIAN MBAPPÉ VS ARGENTINA, 2022

⚽ **With France trailing Argentina 2-1 with just nine minutes of normal time remaining in the final, Les Bleus needed something special, and fast.** Fortunately for Didier Deschamp's side, Mbappé duly delivered. Racing into the Argentina penalty box to receive a lofted pass from Marcus Thuram, Mbappé lashed home an unstoppable first-time volley to drag France level at 2-2, having scored a penalty just a minute before. He would score again in extra time to make it 3-3, a goal that would seal the Golden Boot prize.

MARADONA VS ENGLAND, 1986

⚽ **England were still reeling. Manager Bobby Robson was still remonstrating with anyone who would listen.** Captain Peter Shilton had hardly stopped slapping his arm in protestation at referee Ali Ben Nasser's decision not to blow up. Commentator Barry Davies had only just begun to ascertain that Maradona might have punched – and not headed – the first goal of England's quarter-final against Argentina. But four minutes after the 'Hand of God' had struck, Glenn Hoddle gave the ball away and it was moved to Maradona, some 60 yards from goal. He jinked past Peter Beardsley, turned away from Peter Reid, beat Terry Butcher with sheer speed before utterly bamboozling Terry Fenwick and ghosting past Peter Shilton to score. It took him 11 seconds to score the greatest goal of the tournament.

WORLD CUP LEGENDS

THE MAGNIFICENT MAGYARS

Charting the rise and fall of football's first revolutionary force

Before Klopp's Gegenpress, Spain's Tiki-taka, Cruyff's Total Football and Italy's Catenaccio, there was Hungary's Golden Team. The Magnificent Magyars dominated world football in the 1950s with a revolutionary approach that would change the game forever. They may not be so well remembered as football's other great tactical innovators, but they were no less influential and deserve to be revered as one of the greatest forces the game has ever seen.

Between 1950 and 1956 Hungary racked up an incredible record, winning 42 games, drawing 7 and losing only one, wowing the globe in the 1954 World Cup, where they scored 27 goals in only 5 games. What made them such a formidable force? A large share of the credit must go to the team's innovative coach, Gusztáv Sebes.

When Sebes took charge of Hungary, football's dominant system was the WM formation, or 3-2-2-3. Sebes took a new approach, implementing a 2-3-3-2. It included a revolutionary innovation: the introduction of the deep-lying centre forward. In an era where defenders were wedded to the idea of man-marking, this could play havoc with the opposition, who would often follow the player into midfield and be drawn out of position.

Sebes also implemented a philosophy that was the precursor to Total Football. He wanted his players to be comfortable playing in all positions, ensuring that the side could attack and defend as a unit and that players had the tactical flexibility to be able to interchange with teammates.

Of course, to play in such a style requires a group of talented players, and Hungary were blessed on that front. The team were led by one of the greatest of all time, Ferenc Puskás, who would go on to have a storied career at Real Madrid and who scored an amazing 84 goals in 85 internationals for Hungary. His strike partner wasn't bad either. Sándor Kocsis had a better than a goal a game average, netting 75 goals in 68 appearances for his nation. Behind that prolific duo was more great talent: the man tasked with filling the deep-lying forward role pioneered by Sebes, Nándor Hidegkuti, and skilful left-winger Zoltán Czibor. Josef Bozsik was another key figure. He would sit deep, using his creativity and technique to play in the attacking talent ahead of him.

If this crop of talent wasn't groundbreaking enough, they also had the 'Black Panther', Gyula Grosics. Grosics is credited with being the first sweeper-keeper, pushing up to help mop up attacks and allow his teammates to push deeper into the opponent's half.

Hungary's pioneering group of footballing geniuses set off on a phenomenal run. They went into the 1952 Olympic Games on a two-year unbeaten streak, sweeping defending champions Sweden aside in a 6-0 win and defeating Yugoslavia in the final to claim Olympic gold. The team followed up in 1953 by winning the Central European International Cup.

As the 1954 World Cup drew near, Hungary's growing profile led to them being invited to play in a famous match that provided the perfect illustration of how far ahead they were of other teams: a 1953 friendly against England dubbed the 'Match of the Century'.

England displayed a supreme arrogance coming into the game. Though Hungary were ranked number one in the world, the English football establishment and media felt sure that they would squash these European upstarts. After all, England invented football. Add to that the fact that the game was being played at Wembley, where England had only

THE MAGNIFICENT MAGYARS

○ Hungary legend Ferenc Puskás scores against England in a 7-1 friendly win in 1954

WORLD CUP LEGENDS

"THE TEAM WERE LED BY ONE OF THE GREATEST OF ALL TIME, FERENC PUSKÁS"

been defeated once, and it seemed certain that this eagerly anticipated spectacle would go in their favour.

It didn't. England were dismantled by Hungary in front of their home fans, losing 6-3 in a defeat that shook English football to the core. England were baffled by Hungary's tactical approach, sent into disarray by their fluid positional interchanging. This was exacerbated by the tendency of England's players to base their decisions on who to mark on the numbers their opponents were wearing, rather than the space they were occupying on the pitch. England centre-half Harry Johnston, for example, was accustomed to marking the opposition's centre-forward, the number nine. However, it was Hidegkuti, Sebes' deep-lying forward, who was wearing that number. Johnston was completely bamboozled by Hidegkuti's approach, unsure as to whether he should be sticking with his man and therefore be drawn out of position, or stay where he was and give Hidegkuti the licence to roam free. In short, England were stuck in the past and, confronted by the future, had no idea what to do.

A matter of weeks before the 1954 World Cup in Switzerland, Hungary reinforced their status as the world's best team in a rematch, thrashing England 7-1. Unbeaten since 1950 and with those two hefty wins under their belt, they were the upcoming tournament's clear favourites.

The 1954 tournament had a unique format. There were four groups of four teams, each with two seeded teams and two unseeded teams. Rather than the round-robin format we are used to, seeded teams would only play unseeded teams, meaning there were only four matches in each group.

Hungary were drawn in group two, along with West Germany, Turkey and South Korea. In their first game, Hungary wiped the floor with South Korea, beating them 9-0 thanks to a hat-trick from Kocsis, braces from Puskás and Palotás and goals from Lantos and Czibor. Their second game was against West Germany, who took the risk of fielding a weakened side. They paid for it, losing 8-3. Kocsis was again on form, scoring four, Puskás and Tóth both grabbed a goal and Hidegkuti nabbed two. The defeat didn't end up being too costly for Germany, who qualified for the knockout stages after beating Turkey in a play-off. Hungary, however, had to go into their quarter-final without their star player, Puskás, who was injured in the match.

Hungary met Brazil in the quarter-final. Given that the two teams had a reputation for playing attractive, attacking football - Hungary on their part having already netted 17 goals in two games - the game was expected to be a spectacle. In a sense it was, but not in the way people had anticipated. The infamous match would go down as one of the most violent ever played, earning it the moniker the 'Battle of Berne'.

Despite heavy rain and a slippery pitch, Hungary continued their impressive attacking form early on. In the fourth minute Hidegkuti came out on top in a goalmouth scramble to put Hungary in front. They quickly struck again, Kocsis scoring a header to put them 2-0 up with only eight minutes gone. Both teams started to commit niggly fouls; though the rain continued to hammer down, the temperature of the game was rising. One of those fouls resulted in a penalty for Brazil, which they scored, shifting the momentum in their favour for the rest of the half.

Things really got out of hand in the second half when Hungary were awarded a penalty and Brazilian journalists and officials flooded the pitch in protest. Hungary's Lantos scored

○ The 1954 World Cup final was held in the Wankdorf Stadium and watched by a crowd of 62,000

THE DEMISE OF THE GOLDEN TEAM

The end of the Magnificent Magyars was precipitated by political events at home.

Budapest Honvéd, for whom most of the national team played, were in Spain playing in the European Cup when revolution erupted in Hungary in 1956. The team brought their families out of Hungary and went on a money-raising world tour rather than returning home.

Eventually, some went back, but several key players refused. Kocsis and Czibor, for example, went to play for Barcelona, where both had successful careers. Hungary's star player, Ferenc Puskás, also went to Spain, where he played for Real Madrid for eight seasons, scoring 156 goals in 180 La Liga games. He won La Liga five times in a row between 1961 and 1965, the Spanish Cup once and three European Cups.

With their key players living in exile, the Golden Team was broken apart. In Hungary's next World Cup in 1958 they were eliminated in the group stage.

THE MAGNIFICENT MAGYARS

West Germany's Max Morlock scores his country's first goal in the 1954 World Cup final

WORLD CUP LEGENDS

○ Hungary and Brazil do battle in their notoriously violent World Cup quarter-final clash

THE MAGNIFICENT MAGYARS

the penalty, but the incident further fuelled an already ill-tempered game. Six minutes later Brazil's Nilton Santos put a nasty challenge in on Bozsik. The pair traded punches before being dismissed by the referee.

The reckless tackles and bad blood continued as the match degenerated into a maelstrom of incessant fouling and cynical tactics. In among the chaos Brazil pulled one back to bring the score to 3-2. However, all hopes of levelling the match were extinguished with 11 minutes remaining when Brazil had Humberto sent off for a horror tackle on Lóránt. Hungary's Kocsis then struck again in the 88th minute to give Hungary a 4-2 win.

At the final whistle players and officials became embroiled in an almighty brawl that started on the pitch and continued into the dressing rooms to bring a violent game to a violent conclusion.

Hungary's semi-final match would be against defending champions Uruguay. Uruguay had never lost a World Cup match, having won both the tournaments in which they appeared. Hungary went up against this formidable opponent with their star man Puskás still missing. Even so, they took an early lead in the 13th minute through Czibor, a lead they managed to hold until half time.

Within two minutes of the restart Hungary struck again, this time through Hidegkuti. Uruguay didn't give up though. Instead they played their part in making it a thrilling contest, relentlessly attacking the Hungarian defence. Their persistence paid off in the 75th minute when Hohberg found the net, a feat he would repeat in 86th minute to draw the game level at 2-2.

The match went into extra time, where Hungary's superior fitness saw them take control again. Kocsis struck twice to send Hungary through with another 4-2 win, dealing Uruguay their first World Cup loss in an exciting match that can stake a claim as one of the finest in the tournament's history.

Hungary would meet West Germany in the final, with the result seeming like a forgone conclusion. Hungary hadn't been defeated for four years and had just vanquished the current world champions in the semi-final. Their opponents were not even full professionals, having to work second jobs to get by. Add to that the fact that Hungary had already beaten West Germany 8-3 in the group stages and it seemed certain that the

> **"THE INFAMOUS MATCH WOULD GO DOWN AS ONE OF THE MOST VIOLENT EVER PLAYED"**

Magnificent Magyars would claim the World Cup glory they so obviously deserved.

Despite having not recovered from his injury, Puskás came back into the fold for the final. The decision paid dividends when he bagged the opening goal after six minutes. Czibor followed up only two minutes later, capitalising on a poor backpass. The final was following the script.

However, West Germany quickly struck back. Max Morlock netted from close range in the tenth minute and Rahn scored from a corner in the 19th. Hungary again took the initiative after the equaliser but couldn't find the net and went into the break level.

Hungary kept on attacking after the restart, but a combination of profligacy on their part and sensational goalkeeping on the part of Germany's Turek left them frustrated. Germany's keeper stopped a couple of shots from Puskás and tipped a Kocsis header onto the bar. His compatriot, Kohlmeyer, twice cleared the ball off the line. Then, with six minutes to go, Germany struck.

A high ball into the Hungary box was cleared but dropped to Rahn, who dummied a pass to his centre-forward, ducked into the penalty box and powered a low shot into Hungary's net. The match ended 3-2 to West Germany. Hungary's phenomenal run was over and the defeat would go down in history as one of football's biggest upsets, a match known as the 'Miracle of Berne'.

There were several controversies in the wake of the loss. Some felt Hungary should have been awarded a free kick for a foul on goalkeeper Grosics in the build up to Germany's second goal; Puskás had a goal disallowed in the final minutes of the game; and Kocsis was denied a penalty. There were also allegations about the West Germany side taking performance-enhancing drugs. What made the defeat most painful of all, however, is how much of an aberration it would prove to be. Between its emergence in 1950 and its breaking apart in 1956, this was the only game Hungary's Golden Team lost.

Hungary would never get the World Cup win they deserved. With the coming of the Hungarian Revolution in 1956 the Golden Team were broken up, and the nation would never again reach the same footballing heights. Even so, we should still celebrate the legacy of the team's revolutionary approach to the beautiful game and the legend of its truly incredible players.

HUNGARY FACTS & FIGURES

91% WIN RATIO FROM JUNE 1950 – FEB 1956

ACHIEVED THE JOINT BIGGEST WORLD CUP VICTORY WITH THEIR **9-0** DEFEAT OF SOUTH KOREA

27 MOST GOALS IN A WORLD CUP TOURNAMENT

MOST CONSECUTIVE GAMES SCORING AT LEAST ONE GOAL **73**

STRIKER **SÁNDOR KOCSIS** WAS THE FIRST PLAYER TO SCORE TWO HAT-TRICKS IN A WORLD CUP — **2**

WORLD CUP LEGENDS

MOMENTS
4 JULY 1998

BERGKAMP'S BRILLIANCE

The Dutch master scores one of the World Cup's greatest goals

Dennis Bergkamp has scored no shortage of sensational goals in his career. One of his best was on the global stage that is the World Cup, scored against Argentina in a 1998 quarter-final. Not only was it a fantastic goal in and of itself, but it was scored in the 90th minute to break a 1-1 deadlock and send the Netherlands into the next round at the expense of Argentina. That made an already special goal just a little more special.

The goal is exemplary of Bergkamp's supreme technical skill and footballing intelligence. His first task was to control a raking pass sent from deep inside the Dutch half by Frank de Boer. Stretching for the ball with his right foot while on the run, Bergkamp somehow managed to kill the ball dead. His next task was to beat the defender running alongside him. Bergkamp quickly followed up on his first touch with a delicate flick that brought the ball back inside as he checked his run, taking the defender who had been chasing him out by using his own momentum against him. Bergkamp's third task was to finish. He did it perfectly, stroking the ball with the outside of his foot to send it bending into the far corner. Those three precise touches won the game for the Netherlands and ensured that Bergkamp's name will always be mentioned in the discussion about the greatest World Cup goals.

WORLD CUP LEGENDS

RONALDO
HOW 'O FENÔMENO' WENT FROM WORLD CUP ZERO TO HERO

Ronaldo never felt worse than after the 1998 final. Four years later, he would have turned it all around

There is a period of football with which Ronaldo will always be synonymous. In the late 1990s and early 2000s, he was named FIFA World Player of the Year three times. Twice he picked up the Ballon d'Or. One achievement will always rank above the rest, though: his redemptive and emotional World Cup victory in 2002, when he finally helped Brazil back to the top of world football.

However, to fully understand the gravity and enormity of that peak, you must first comprehend the depth of his trough.

Ronaldo had been present at the 1994 World Cup, bookended by two penalty misses: Diana Ross's in the opening ceremony and Roberto Baggio's in the final shootout. The latter had handed Dunga's Brazil their fourth global crown, and Ronaldo had been one of those sprinting onto the field in celebration. But the 17-year-old Cruzeiro striker only featured as an unused substitute in the tournament, and probably felt like he was gatecrashing the victory party. By the time France '98 swung around four years later, he had become the poster boy for Brazil's title defence, and carried the hopes of a nation.

The expectation on a Seleção going into any World Cup cannot be overstated. When Brazil were beaten by Uruguay in a home 1950 World Cup final, three fans present died from heart attacks and one even took his own life. The yellow and green shirts they wear now were only adopted after they abandoned the white ones they had worn on that day. The defeat was a national tragedy. It is still spoken about in hushed, embarrassed voices.

That is the weight that was being born on Ronaldo's 21-year-old shoulders. Now, there was little doubting that in footballing terms, they were more than broad enough to bear them. He had already netted 25 times for his

RONALDO

○ Ronaldo ended the 2002 World Cup as top scorer with eight goals

WORLD CUP LEGENDS

country, and perhaps most impressively 19 of those came outside Brazil. He had moved to PSV Eindhoven after the 1994 World Cup, and after 54 goals in 57 games, been snapped up by Barcelona. It hadn't been plain sailing – he broke the world transfer record for the second time in a year when contract talks broke down at Barça – but he had settled in well at Inter Milan, and become the best player in the world, as his 1997 Ballon d'Or and FIFA World Player of the Year awards showed.

But he had experienced nothing like being the poster boy for a World Cup. A Cup Winners' Cup final with Barcelona would pale into insignificance. Even the $180 million sponsorship deal he signed with Nike could not match it. The Brazilian team were overflowing with talent and experience, the likes of Roberto Carlos and Rivaldo coming close to challenging Ronaldo for global honours, while Dunga, Cafu and goalkeeper Cláudio Taffarel had all appeared in the 1994 final. But Ronaldo was the jewel in the crown. Everything revolved around him.

The tournament began well for Brazil and for Ronaldo. The Inter striker was his uncontainable self against Scotland, and Ronaldo scored his first World Cup goal in a 3-0 win over Morocco that guaranteed Brazil's top spot in the group. There followed a blip. For the second time in 12 months, Brazil were beaten by Norway, who scored twice in the last seven minutes to put themselves into the second round. "We lost at the right time," Brazil boss Mário Zagallo said. More crucially, they were through to face Chile, whom they had beaten 4-0 a little over 12 months previous, with Ronaldo scoring twice. History nearly repeated itself as Ronaldo scored a penalty that he had won, and added a second 18 minutes from time to seal a 4-1 win.

The wins started to flow: a hard-fought 3-2 win over Denmark, a shootout victory over the Netherlands, and soon Brazil had fulfilled the minimum requirement of their tournament by reaching the final. Anything less would have been an abject failure.

Ronaldo's form was stunning, with four goals and many more moments of magic. There was a chested one-two pass to Cafu against Norway that you'd accuse of showboating if someone did it in five-a-side. There were two more moments, almost carbon-copies of each other, against Denmark and Scotland, where he got the ball out wide of the penalty area with his back to the goal, and the defender assumed he had the situation under control. The ball ended up in the six-yard box inside five seconds.

So more than ever, Ronaldo was pivotal to Brazil's hopes in the final against hosts France, who had in their ranks the only player who could compare to him: Zinedine Zidane.

On the day of the final, an evening kick-off, the Brazilian players went for a customary sleep after lunch. Before Ronaldo's head had even touched the pillow, his roommate, Roberto Carlos, started screaming. 21-year-old Ronaldo was having a fit, frothing at the mouth and convulsing wildly. "I was unconscious for three, four minutes," Ronaldo admitted, years later. "Nobody knows [why]. When you're there, you breathe the competition, everything is about the competition, you cannot disconnect from the competition. It's a lot of pressure."

ONE WORLD CUP TOO FAR

For a man who has scored more goals at a World Cup than all bar one man – his 15 is only beaten by Miroslav Klose's tally of 16 – the 2006 World Cup in Germany was in some ways a bizarre way for Ronaldo to bow out.

Although he was only just approaching 30, the twilight of his career was clearly upon him. The knee injuries from which he had remarkably recovered in 2002 would not go away, and neither would his ever-expanding waistline.

In their final group game, Ronaldo showed flashes of his old self, with a no-look pass that nearly set up the opener, a headed equaliser and a booming finish from the edge of the box to seal a 4-1 win over Japan. Against Ghana in the last 16 too, he beat the goalkeeper with a vintage stepover – but it was to be his last goal at a World Cup.

When Brazil faced France in the quarter-finals, he was off the pace and lacklustre, only finally testing goalkeeper Fabien Barthez in stoppage time after a sub-par 90 minutes. Overweight and underperforming, it was the last time we would see Ronaldo at the very highest level.

RONALDO

"ROBERTO CARLOS HAD STARTED SCREAMING AND RONALDO WAS FROTHING AT THE MOUTH"

Ronaldo was on top of his game throughout the 2002 World Cup, scoring in every game apart from the quarter-final against England

97

WORLD CUP LEGENDS

Ronaldo's illness in the 1998 final was seen as a national injustice in Brazil and the beaten finalists were warmly welcomed home

"IN A FRONT THREE WITH RIVALDO AND RONALDINHO, RONALDO TERRORISED DEFENCES IN 2002"

After the fit, Ronaldo slept soundly, but when he awoke, he was taken to hospital while the rest of the players, all of whom had been disturbed by the shouting and screaming, headed to the stadium, their minds firmly on Ronaldo - and not France.

Just 40 minutes before kick-off, Ronaldo was hastily added to the team-sheet and he was back to fulfil his destiny. The players later admitted their concerns about whether he was fully fit, and if his performance was anything to go by, he wasn't. Ronaldo lacked the precision and flair that had characterised his tournament, and while defending was not his forte, his allowing Zidane to ghost into the area and head home was indicative of a mental state far from focused.

In the wake of the 3-0 defeat and mysterious goings-on of the afternoon, Brazil launched a full-scale inquiry. Players, coaches and doctors all gave evidence, but the lack of explanation for the fit sparked conspiracy theories galore. Some claimed he had reacted badly to a pain injection to deal with an ongoing knee problem; others that Nike had pressured Brazil to let him play despite not being fit to do so. Only one thing was certain: Ronaldo was flying home without a World Cup winners' medal and would have to wait four long years to right the wrongs.

Fast forward that intervening period, and Brazil could hardly have found themselves in a more contrasting situation to the one that preceded the 1998 World Cup. 'O Fenômeno' - the Italian press coined the nickname and the Brazilians adopted it - tore a knee ligament in April 2000. It had taken the best part of two years to get over it - he did not play a single game for Inter in the 2000-01 season. Without him, Brazil's qualifying campaign had been uninspiring, losing more than two matches in the competition for the first time ever; six out of 18 in all.

Ronaldo did score once ahead of the tournament, a strike in a friendly against Malaysia being his first goal for Brazil in two and a half years.

RONALDO

his head in an effort to deflect attention from the problem, had seemingly faded. Now all they had to do was beat Germany in the final.

But now Brazil also had to take on the nerves and the pressure. Everything that was true four years ago was true now: a nation expected. Hours before the final, unable to ignore the fact that four years ago his world had been turned upside down, Ronaldo was starting to feel nervous again.

"After lunch everyone went for a sleep and to do their stuff," he explained. "I was looking for people to talk to – I didn't want to go to sleep! I found Dida, the goalkeeper, and he talked to me the whole time until we left for the stadium. I was very scared."

You wouldn't have known it. Lining up before the anthems, Ronaldo and Ronaldinho can be seen laughing with each other, apparently not out of nerves but genuine enjoyment of the moment. When the football started, their interplay was brilliant. Twice before half-time, they combined to leave Ronaldo one-on-one with Oliver Kahn, but neither time could he beat the keeper. After a third gilt-edged opportunity was blocked, he shook his head with a look that said, 'it's happening again'.

After the break, the balance started to shift, and the German front two of Miroslav Klose and Oliver Neuville came closer to breaking the deadlock. Ronaldo's body language grew worse, but his striker's instinct never left him. After winning the ball back in the opposition half, he followed up Rivaldo's shot and scored a poacher's goal when Kahn spilled it.

If that goal was fortunate, the second was pure quality. Rivaldo dummied over a pass from Kléberson, and Ronaldo's finish was pinpoint accurate. His eighth goal of the World Cup came 11 minutes from time – Germany could not respond. Manager Luiz Felipe Scolari took him off in the last minute so he could receive a mighty standing ovation.

And when the final whistle sounded, where four years ago he had stood lost and alone with the weight of expectation too much for his young shoulders, the flag of Brazil adorned them this time, and his smile was overwhelmingly one of relief. The greatest footballer in the world had won the greatest trophy – and justice had been done.

But he did not even need time to grow into his new knee and new, larger body. Even after so long out, he was no less potent. He scored in every group game, terrorising China, Costa Rica and Turkey, along with Rivaldo and Ronaldinho in a formidable front three.

Just like the 1998 final, Brazil's entire World Cup preparation had been focused around a Ronaldo injury, only this time, it had all come together. The stars seemed, finally, to be aligning. Even England, whose golden generation appeared to be delivering a return to the big time their country had so longed for, fell foul of a sliced Ronaldinho free-kick that freakishly beat David Seaman and secured a semi-final berth against Turkey. There was an element of fortune about that win, too; Ronaldo's shot somehow evading Rüştü Reçber in the Turkish goal, despite its apparent lack of power. The groin injury that had caused him, he claims, to shave part of

RONALDO FACTS & FIGURES

SECOND-HIGHEST SCORER IN WORLD CUP HISTORY WITH 15 GOALS

TWICE BROKE WORLD TRANSFER RECORD BEFORE HIS 21ST BIRTHDAY

47 GOALS IN ONE SEASON FOR BARCELONA

FIFTH FOREIGNER TO SCORE 100 GOALS FOR REAL MADRID

62 INTERNATIONAL GOALS IN 98 APPEARANCES

ONLY BRAZILIAN TO WIN TWO BALLON D'ORS

WORLD CUP LEGENDS

TOP 10: KITS

The most vibrant, memorable and iconic kits sported by the legends and minnows on the world's greatest stage

USA, 1994

Almost everyone hated the garish away kit the USA team wore on home soil at the 1994 World Cup, at least at first. Who, after all, would want a denim-style football shirt? However, it grew on people and that blue-and-white jersey is now something of a cult classic.

ITALY, 1978

We had to include one of the kits worn by the team nicknamed after the colour it wears, the Azzurri. This classic version from 1978 doesn't overcomplicate things. All you need is that rich blue, a simple badge with the green, white and red of the Italian flag and some white shorts.

WEST GERMANY, 1990

It's no coincidence that some of the World Cup's most iconic kits are worn by its most successful teams. Adding to the traditional plain white of previous kits, West Germany's 1990 version received an injection of colour with these cool angular stripes in the red, yellow and black of the German flag. It was the last kit worn before reunification brought East and West Germany together.

NETHERLANDS, 1978

The famous kit of the Netherlands national team and the accompanying wall of orange their supporters bring to any tournament they are involved in is one of the great sights of the World Cup. We've picked out the kit that the team wore on their way to defeat to Argentina in the 1978 World Cup final, with its chunky black badge and sleeve stripes to accompany the classic colour.

ARGENTINA, 1986

Wearing this classic iteration of the blue-and-white striped Argentina jersey, Diego Maradona would lead his country to World Cup glory, defeating West Germany 3-2 in the final. The brilliant yellow of the badge contrasts nicely with the muted blue and white of the shirt.

TOP 10: KITS

ZAIRE, 1974

⚽ **The Zaire team of 1974 were not good.** They were beaten 9-0 by Yugoslavia in the group stage and finished bottom with 0 points. Had they got further, this fantastic shirt would surely be better remembered. With a picture of a leopard attacking a football emblazoned on the front, we think it's one of the coolest kits in football history.

ENGLAND, 1966

⚽ **White may be England's traditional colour when it comes to its football kits, but its most iconic shirt is easily the red one that the team wore in the 1966 World Cup final.** Everybody knows that famous image of Bobby Moore lifting the Jules Rimet Trophy high in that very kit. It is proof that the simple ones are sometimes the best: a plain red shirt with the three lions badge on the chest.

CROATIA, 1998

⚽ **Croatia put in a surprisingly impressive showing at their first World Cup in 1998, finishing third, in no small part thanks to the goals of their prolific striker, Davor Šuker.** Their striking chequered red-and-white kit is one of the most memorable in the competition's history.

DENMARK, 1986

⚽ **Denmark made their World Cup debut with a striking kit design, half thin, red-and-white stripes and half a block of white.** With the chevrons on the sleeves, the black collar and red shorts, there's quite a lot going on, but it works.

BRAZIL, 1982

⚽ **Is there a more iconic shirt in football than the vibrant yellow worn by the World Cup's most successful nation?** We think not. Brazil's stylish kits have become synonymous with the sumptuous football its teams have delighted us with, and the supreme talent of the incredible players that have worn it over the ages. Indeed, we could have filled this list with beautiful Brazil kits, but we've decided to top it with the best of all. The 1982 World Cup was not Brazil's most successful - it had an unusual two-group format, with Brazil eliminated in the second group phase - but they still treated us to some amazing football, led by legends Zico and Sócrates. The tournament also gave us a stunner of a kit. Brazil's classic yellow shirt was set off by green trim on the sleeves and collar and complemented by those brilliant blue shorts and white socks.

101

WORLD CUP LEGENDS

○ Franz Beckenbauer holds the new World Cup trophy aloft in 1974 as West Germany become champions for the second time

FRANZ BECKENBAUER
THE ORIGINAL BECKS

The footballer nicknamed 'Der Kaiser' led West Germany to glory in 1974 in more ways than one

In the summer of 1974, West Germany manager Helmut Schön - the man who had led the team in two previous World Cup campaigns - was clearly at his wit's end. Before him in the heavily guarded training camp in rural Malente was a bunch of players bored out of their minds, fed up with constant supervision, and in open dispute over the bonus payments they should receive if they won the World Cup.

It was that latter point that upset Schön the most. He believed playing for West Germany was an honour, and he was so angry that he even threatened to replace the lot of them with a bunch of reserves. Luckily for the team's star names, it didn't come to that and West Germany went on to lift the trophy. But this apparent miracle was less to do with Schön's mastermind tactics and more to do with the growing influence and talent of one player. Indeed, there is no doubt that 1974 was Franz Beckenbauer's year.

Beckenbauer was West Germany's pioneering defender, and 1974 should always have been his golden chance to shine. The country was hosting the tournament that summer, and it was felt that having a home advantage would ease them over the line just as it had done in previous years for Uruguay, Italy and England. By that point, the Germans had established a fierce footballing reputation. Yet the issues they faced pre-tournament threatened to knock their status as one of the strong favourites.

Still, West Germany and Beckenbauer had learned much over the previous eight years. The defender's calm and composed style of play had been very much in evidence at the 1966 World Cup. There, football fans saw his preference to play the ball on the ground, while glimpsing his equal strength when dealing with balls in the air. He was also a tough tackler, taking games by the scruff of the neck when need be, his passion for victory more than evident.

Certainly, his stature and undoubted skill were why opposing teams would do all they could to nullify him. England midfielder Bobby Charlton spent the 1966 final following him around the pitch at Wembley on what would be a disappointing day for Beckenbauer both personally and as a team (England recorded their famous World Cup-winning victory). Rather than become despondent, however, Beckenbauer went on to revolutionise the game.

Arguably the greatest contribution that Beckenbauer went on to make was single-handedly cementing the role of the attacking sweeper, or the *libero* as it was also known. He believed his club team, Bayern Munich, was too cavalier and he strove to be more efficient. His role would see him 'sweeping up' the ball if an opponent managed to breach the defensive line, and it ensured his play was more fluid. In one fell swoop, he'd transformed a traditional defensive position and become an attacking defender. Such skills proved vital in the World Cup.

The first time anyone saw this at a tournament was in 1970, when West Germany started well, winning their three group matches thanks to a tremendous display by striker Gerd Müller. They went on to exact revenge against England by beating the champions 3-2 after extra time, but they came unstuck against Italy 4-3, again after extra time, in the semis, eventually making do with third place.

Nevertheless, West Germany had become feared. With Beckenbauer appointed captain, they went into the 1972 European Championship in Belgium along with just three other teams: Belgium, the Soviet Union and Hungary. West Germany won not only their two games but the tournament. It was good practice for 1974, but it also came on the back of a lengthy period of domestic success for Beckenbauer, who had excelled throughout his footballing life.

Born in post-war Munich in 1945, Beckenbauer had joined SC München von 1906 aged nine. Five years later, when it

WORLD CUP LEGENDS

BECKENBAUER FACTS & FIGURES

- 14 INTERNATIONAL GOALS
- COMPETED IN 3 FIFA WORLD CUP TOURNAMENTS
- 103 APPEARANCES FOR WEST GERMANY
- WON THE WORLD CUP TWICE ONCE AS A PLAYER ONCE AS A MANAGER
- HIS WIN PERCENTAGE AS MANAGER OF WEST GERMANY WAS 51.52%

---

became apparent his club was struggling to finance the youth team, he signed for Bayern Munich and made his debut on 6 June 1964 against Stuttgarter Kickers. He went on to establish himself in a strong 1960s side and arguably became Germany's first footballing 'pop star', the original Becks so to speak. The trophies also just kept coming.

First was the German Cup in 1966, followed by the European Cup Winners' Cup in 1967. There was another German Cup win in 1968, the year he was made captain of Bayern and crowned 'Der Kaiser' by the *Süddeutsche Zeitung* newspaper. He repaid the faith being put in him during the 1968-69 season, when he helped his team to their first Bundesliga. With 18 wins, ten draws and six losses, Bayern Munich's 46 points put them eight ahead of second-place Alemannia Aachen.

Success continued. In 1974, Bayern Munich had completed the continental double, winning the Bundesliga by a point over Borussia Mönchengladbach and the European Cup in a replay against Atlético Madrid. That was Beckenbauer's fourth league victory and he had also won the German Cup four times by this point. As a major footballing world star and the most important player in the West German team, he also had an agent, a string of adverts behind him and even a hit song. He was at the pinnacle of his career.

Unfortunately for both Beckenbauer and West Germany, however, there was another team receiving plaudits for their talent and play. The Dutch team of 1974 were openly compared to The Beatles thanks to their penchant for playing Total Football and the sheer number of stars in their squad, chief among them Johan Cruyff. Just as with Beckenbauer, there was a worldwide fascination with Cruyff. Maarten de Vos made a film about his life called *Number 14* and he'd won the Ballon d'Or two years running – actually pipping Beckenbauer (the 1972 winner) in 1974.

As such, there was something of a competitive edge between the two players, but Beckenbauer had developed a real knack for being able to proactively read the game. If he lost the ball, he would be able to reactively win it back, no matter who had it. His spatial awareness was also second to none, and his decision-making was impeccable.

All of these skills would stand him in good stead for the weeks that lay ahead of him in

> "THERE IS NO DOUBT THAT 1974 WAS FRANZ BECKENBAUER'S YEAR"

1974. And so it was that the West Germans beat Chile 1-0 in the opening match before 81,100 fans at the Olympiastadion in West Berlin, and smashed three past Australia at the Volksparkstadion in Hamburg four days later. It wasn't a great performance, however, and Beckenbauer even spat towards the crowd when he was criticised for giving the ball away. "I'm so sorry," he said afterwards, as fans and the press expressed concern that the pre-tournament turmoil was affecting the team's performances on the pitch.

The problem came to a head in a match against a team so very close to home: East Germany. The German Democratic Republic, as it was formally known, had never qualified for the World Cup before, and it was the first time the two countries had met in a professional match since the division of 1949. It was always going to be a troublesome game, politically if nothing else, given the ongoing Cold War. But while West Germany's quality should have outshone their communist neighbours, it just didn't work out that way.

In truth, the game had little impact on either team's progression to the next round. Earlier that same day – 22 June 1974 – Australia had drawn against Chile, so neither German team were in danger of being knocked out. With political tensions high on both sides of the Berlin Wall, however, all eyes were on both sets of players. Schön certainly felt the pressure.

But then there was much to fear. Most of the East German side was made up of FC Magdeburg players – a team that had beaten AC Milan 2-0 in the European Cup Winners' Cup that year. So while the West Germans were, at heart, Bayern Munich, there was some relief that the frustrating first half proved inconclusive. It wasn't to last. East German Jürgen Sparwasser got on the end of a long-ball that soared over the head of a pointing Beckenbauer, sped past three fumbling West German defenders and smashed it into the back of the net. East Germany won 1-0 and topped the group.

Schön was flattened to the point where he wouldn't even speak, and the mood became as depressing as the miserable wet weather that had descended upon the country for this tournament. But it proved surprisingly pivotal for Beckenbauer, who virtually held his boss's hand throughout the rest of the tournament,

FRANZ BECKENBAUER

○ Franz Beckenbauer scored twice against Switzerland in his first World Cup tournament match for West Germany in 1966

○ Despite England's best efforts, West Germany beat them 3-2 in the 1970 World Cup quarter-final

WORLD CUP LEGENDS

○ West Germany captain Franz Beckenbauer clatters into the Dutchman Johan Neeskens in the 1974 World Cup final

FRANZ BECKENBAUER

"THE TROPHY WAS HIS AT THE THIRD TIME OF ASKING"

becoming greatly influential. Players would go to him for guidance and they'd urge him to persuade Schön to change his tactics.

Coming second in their group actually worked well for West Germany, since they ended up in a relatively straightforward second group stage. West Germany beat Yugoslavia 2-0, Sweden 4-2 and Poland 1-0 and topped the group, while East Germany struggled against the Netherlands, Argentina and Brazil. Even so, none of the West German performances had really blown the supporters away. In fact, they were unimpressed by the negative approach. To make matters worse, it was very obvious that Schön was having a difficult time, mentally. Beckenbauer attended subsequent press conferences with him and spoke about the tactics and the games. Schön sought Beckenbauer's input and took his ideas on board. Uli Hoeneß was dropped to the bench for the Yugoslavia match on Beckenbauer's suggestion.

As can be imagined, it was a highly unusual state of affairs. Meanwhile, the Netherlands – who stormed through both groups with five victories and just one draw – were impressing everyone with a noticeable swagger on and off the pitch. The two camps were like chalk and cheese but, as Beckenbauer told the German weekly news magazine *Der Spiegel* in 2006, "We took a long time in 1974 to find our feet." Even so, he maintains it was a good side. The fact they ended up in the final against the Netherlands was mighty proof of that.

At stake was the new FIFA World Cup trophy. The Jules Rimet had been retained by Brazil in 1970, and both sides were eager to kickstart the new era. Johan Neeskens smashed home a penalty for the Netherlands after just two minutes and the crowd at the Olympiastadion, Munich, could have been forgiven for thinking West Germany would be overrun. But no. Paul Breitner equalised on 25 minutes for West Germany and Gerd Müller scored in the 43rd minute. Johan Cruyff was booked for arguing with the referee at half time and West Germany held firm.

No matter how hard the Netherlands pressed Beckenbauer, the German's passing remained perfect and he opened up space for his teammates. He was so effective that the Dutch ripped up their pre-planned tactics and sought to minimise Beckenbauer's effectiveness on the ball with strong defending. They let him play in his own half but looked to stop him in theirs, but the deep defending went against everything the Dutch appeared to stand for. The final became synonymous with Beckenbauer instead and the trophy was his at the third time of asking. What's more, it was in the city of his birth.

Beckenbauer retired from international football three years later, in 1977. During that time, he won the European Cup with Bayern Munich two more times and supplemented that with the Intercontinental Cup in 1976. West Germany lost the final of the European Championship in 1976, but Beckenbauer was not only the German Footballer of the Year that year but also the winner once again of the prestigious Ballon d'Or. His legendary status was confirmed.

BECKENBAUER: THE CHAMPION MANAGER

After leaving Bayern Munich in 1977 – the year he retired from international football – Beckenbauer went on to play for the New York Cosmos. He then returned to compete in the Bundesliga with Hamburger SV (for whom he won the title) and had one last spell in the Big Apple before hanging up his football boots.

But of all his roles in the wake of that 1974 World Cup, the one that sticks in everyone's mind is that of manager of the West Germany team. He was handed the managerial reins of his country in 1984, and his impact was certainly swift.

He took West Germany to the 1986 World Cup final, losing only to an Argentina side packing the skills of Diego Maradona. He then went straight to the final in 1990 and, on Italian soil, revenged the previous result by managing his side to a World Cup victory courtesy of an 85th-minute penalty by Andreas Brehme. Even then, having tasted World Cup success both as a player and a manager, his involvement with the greatest tournament on in the world didn't end. He headed the successful bid by Germany to organise the FIFA World Cup in 2006. Unfortunately for him, Germany could only manage third place on that occasion.

WORLD CUP LEGENDS

SPAIN'S TIKI-TAKA REVOLUTION

Spain winning on a global stage changed the way the game was played forever

We've all been there. You're about to get on a long flight and there's one group of guys who think it's hilarious to have a few too many drinks beforehand, and start doing the conga up and down the aisle even before you've taken off. For a couple of hundred people on the way back from South Africa in 2010, that was the case with 23 young Spanish men. The difference was that they had just won the World Cup. So they were cut a little slack.

The story of that triumph in South Africa goes back years, and features perennial disappointment for a country steeped in football history. Two of the world's greatest teams reside in Spain, with Real Madrid and Barcelona featuring as key players in the story of the game, but on the world stage, Spain had been an extra in the modern era.

After finishing fourth in 1950, they had failed to qualify for four of the next six editions and would not make the knockout stages until 1986 - a run that included winning just one game at their home competition in 1982.

"This cup, this triumph is for all of you, and for the whole Spanish football factory," Spain coach Vicente del Bosque bellowed to a massive crowd in central Madrid - even though at the heart of this most Spanish victory, there was a Dutchman at Barcelona to thank for its inception.

Johan Cruyff is recognised as one of the greatest players of all time, but it was his eight-year spell as Barcelona manager that left its most permanent mark on the footballing world in the 2010 World Cup.

He engendered his philosophy of possession football and constantly being available for a pass throughout Barcelona and it stuck, so that when Spaniards Xavi and Andrés Iniesta graduated from La Masia,

SPAIN'S TIKI-TAKA REVOLUTION

"THIS CUP, THIS TRIUMPH IS FOR ALL OF YOU, AND FOR THE WHOLE SPANISH FOOTBALL FACTORY"

David Villa and Sergio Ramos lift the trophy as the Spain team celebrate victory at the 2010 World Cup

And yet within one game, they were in tatters. Their midfield, despite overflowing with talent, could not find a way past Switzerland's Diego Benaglio, and seven minutes into the second half, Manchester City reject Gelson Fernandes scored one of the great scrappy goals after it pinballed off two Spanish defenders and Iker Casillas.

Spain had 22 shots on goal, a stat they nearly matched in their second group game against Honduras – but on that occasion, their 19 efforts did at least herald two goals, even if profligacy was a running theme. David Villa grabbed them both.

"He has scored whenever he wants," Del Bosque would say ahead of the semi-final. That wasn't quite true. He should have scored at least four against Honduras, missing from the spot. Perfection was still a distance away.

The final group game had plenty riding on it, with the runner-up in Group H facing Brazil in the second round. It was a keen sword of Damocles to hang over a game between two sides who knew each other well, and Marcelo Bielsa's Chile seemed unlikely to roll over without a fight.

But for once, luck was on Spain's side. A goalkeeping blunder and a controversial red card for Chile's Marco Estrada helped them secure a 2-1 win, and Spain were through.

the famous Barça academy, they were fully fledged disciples of the Cruyff way. They had seen his Dream Team win the league four times in a row and wanted to take that success to the biggest stage in the world.

For Xavi, 2010 was his third bite of the cherry; Iniesta, his second. Barça's 2009 Champions League victory with Cruyff apostle Guardiola in charge and Xavi, Iniesta, Gerard Piqué, Carles Puyol, Víctor Valdés and Sergio Busquets all starting the final was a good sign. The 2008 European Championship win and a 35-match unbeaten run that ended in 2009 were very good signs.

WORLD CUP LEGENDS

It set up their sternest test yet: a clash with Cristiano Ronaldo's Portugal. And the goal that put the Real Madrid star out was Barcelona through and through. Iniesta played a delicate pass between two defenders into Xavi's feet, who flicked the ball off the outside of his foot into the path of Villa who, with an hour gone, produced a familiar and decisive finish.

The same scoreline - 1-0 Spain, Villa - saw them dispatch Paraguay to move into the last four. On paper, Spain weren't vintage; Villa's winner coming seven minutes from the end. They were winning while not thrashing sides, but one flash of brilliance every 90 minutes was proving enough. Just.

It is not the sort of form in which you want to find yourselves against World Cup semi-final regulars Germany. They had put four past England and Argentina in the previous rounds and were the exciting team of the tournament. But Spain just kept winning 1-0, doing so for the third time in a row to reach a first-ever final.

The fact was that Spain were keeping the ball so much that sides were left with precious little opportunity to score for themselves. Against Germany, Spain had 61 per cent possession. Against Paraguay, 62. In defeat to Switzerland, it was 67. It was the Barcelona-Cruyff training in action: be available, want the ball, keep the ball. No one passed the ball more than Xavi, Xabi Alonso and Sergio Busquets in the 2010 World Cup. If you have the ball, the other team can't score.

And had Spain's finishing been even a little better, the story of the 2010 World Cup might have been an even more dominant one. The 1-0 wins on paper may appear meagre, but in fact, Spain's quality was so high that a narrow win was the floor rather than the ceiling of their performance.

But it required an immense level of quality from every player to do so, and attacking players who could unpick defences from settled positions, where disciplined defenders would not be pulled around.

It seemed fitting that a style based so much around playing the perfect game of football - where the winning side would keep the ball at all times - would come up against one that was ultimately pragmatic in the final.

Just as José Mourinho's Inter Milan midfield of Esteban Cambiasso and Thiago Motta had won the Champions League that year, so the Netherlands had Mark van Bommel and Nigel de Jong.

The Dutch side tried to impose themselves physically on the relatively diminutive Spaniards. One of the abiding memories of the final was de Jong kicking Alonso in the chest, but failing to be shown the red card. English referee Howard Webb regards that game, in which he was forced to show 14 yellow cards and one red, as one of the toughest of his life.

Soccer City and its 84,490 fans were in the end treated, as they often had been by Spain, to just one moment of real quality. And it was fitting that it was Iniesta who produced it. Found by fellow La Masia graduate Cesc Fàbregas in the box, he hit a bouncing ball into the far corner with just four minutes of extra time remaining. Spain were spared penalties, their enemy before and during the 2010 World Cup, and history beckoned them with open arms.

Xabi Alonso of Spain (left) is fouled by Nigel de Jong of the Netherlands

David Villa of Spain misses a goal-scoring chance as goalkeeper Maarten Stekelenburg of the Netherlands dives to save

JOHAN CRUYFF, THE FATHER OF TIKI-TAKA

As a player at Barcelona, Cruyff won La Liga, the Ballon d'Or and was the Golden Ball winner of 1974. But it is as a coach that the Spaniards of the 21st century came to know his name so prominently. "Nothing in football would be possible without the arrival and the unequalled charisma and talent of Johan Cruyff," Pep Guardiola has said.

When Cruyff took over as Barcelona boss, already a league winner there as a player, they had finished sixth in the league the year before and won La Liga just once in 15 years. It is a testament to his success that he left eight years later having championed Spain four times and Europe once.

But equally, his revolution was not an instant or an obvious one. "I'm never afraid of making mistakes and I tried to bring that idea to the pitch," Cruyff said. "I told players not to be afraid: 'If you have an idea, good: try it. And if it goes wrong, don't worry.'"

His ideology was a simple one: that football should be studied, analysed and played in an innovative and attacking way, with every player on the field contributing to keeping the ball. No player at the club, top to bottom, was exempt from his revolution.

"If we want things to change, we must change history," he said on his arrival as manager. He would shape the future too, at Barcelona and all over Spain.

WORLD CUP LEGENDS

MOMENTS
8 JULY 2014

KILLING THE DREAM

Germany send Brazil crashing out of the World Cup with a 7-1 thrashing

Brazil weren't in an ideal state coming into their semi-final match against Germany in the 2014 World Cup. Their star player, Neymar, had been injured in the previous game against Colombia and captain Thiago Silva was suspended. Still, Brazil were going into the match undefeated and were playing on home soil. It was expected to be a close game.

What followed was a humiliation dubbed the *Mineirazo*, a reference to Brazil's shock defeat in the 1950 World Cup final, also played on home soil, known as the *Maracanazo*. Brazil were a mess and were comfortably dismantled by a German team, who would go on to win the tournament.

Müller struck first, converting from a corner after he was allowed to go unmarked in the box. Then, in an incredible six minutes, Brazil collapsed as Germany netted four goals to destroy their World Cup hopes. Klose scored in the 23rd minute to take his total World Cup tally to 16, overtaking the all-time top-scorer record held by Brazil's Ronaldo. Kroos then drilled one in with his left from the edge of the box in the 24th minute and slotted a tap-in home in the 26th. Khedira popped up to give Germany a 5-0 lead in the 29th minute that they took into the half-time break. Schürrle came on in the second half to net another two, the second a thunderous strike into the near top corner. Brazil could only grab a consolation in the 90th minute through Oscar to bring an embarrassing, but entertaining, 7-1 defeat to a close.

WORLD CUP LEGENDS

TOP 10: FUTURE LEGENDS

Who are the next generation of World Cup legends? We try to predict the future

PEDRI

⚽ **"He reminds me a lot of Andrés Iniesta. If we're talking about pure talent, Pedri is the best prospect in the world".** When Xavi sees flashes of his former midfield partner in a player, you know they must be pretty special, and Barcelona's 19-year-old playmaker certainly belongs in that category. The driving force behind Spain's run to the EURO 2020 semi-finals, Pedri won Young Player of the Tournament. Already a fixture for club and country, he will be crucial to La Roja's chances of success in future tournaments.

VINÍCIUS JÚNIOR

⚽ **To stand out on the streets of Brazil requires skill, tenacity and unwavering self-belief.** Marry all that with a beaming grin and a humble attitude and you've got quite the player, which is precisely what Real Madrid thought when they snapped up a 16-year-old Vinícius Júnior for £38 million. Since his move to Spain in July 2018 he has won two league titles, scored the winner in a Champions League final and established himself in Brazil's national set up. He bagged two assists in an otherwise disappointing 2022 World Cup campaign for Brazil, but with time and talent on his side, he could well take his country much further in 2026.

JUDE BELLINGHAM

⚽ **Hailed as one of the finest young players in the world, Bellingham began his stratospheric ascent to Europe's top table as an Under-8 at Birmingham City.** Rising through the ranks at speed, he became the Blues' youngest first-team player ever at just 16. Courted by numerous clubs, in July 2020 he elected to move to Borussia Dortmund, where he blossomed into a magnificent midfielder. The youngest English player ever to feature at a major tournament, he shone in Qatar with a goal against Iran and an assist against Senegal. It's no surprise Real Madrid were willing to spend £88 million to secure the signature of a player destined to run England's midfield for years to come.

CHARLES DE KETELAERE

⚽ **Quick turn of pace? Check.** Able to spin out of a challenge? No problem. Can drift between the lines undetected? All the time. Six foot three? Lanky frontmen seemed destined to become a thing of seasons past, but if De Ketelaere's career to date is any barometer, goal-bothering beanpoles are back in fashion. AC Milan will certainly hope that's the case, as will Belgium.

JULIÁN ÁLVAREZ

⚽ **The hype surrounding Erling Haaland's move to Manchester City saw this skilful Argentinean slip under the radar, but Premier League defences have since learnt about 'the Spider'.** Able to play anywhere across a front three, Álvarez was superb in Qatar, scoring four goals, including a brace against Croatia in the semi-finals. Messi might be approaching the end of his career, but La Albiceleste won't struggle for goals with this guy around.

TOP 10: FUTURE LEGENDS

ALPHONSO DAVIES

⚽ **The son of Liberian refugees, Davies was born in a refugee camp in Ghana but fled the continent with his family and crossed the Atlantic to Canada.** Snapped up by the Whitecaps at 14, the lightning-fast left-back made such an impression in the MLS that German giants Bayern Munich moved quickly to secure his signature in 2018. An international stalwart at just 22, he played a vital role in helping Canada to reach just its second World Cup.

JAMAL MUSIALA

⚽ **A product of Chelsea's superb academy, Jamal Musiala signed for Bayern in July 2019 at 16 years of age.** A former England youth player, since switching his allegiance to Germany he has amassed 23 international caps and one goal. Capable of playing anywhere in midfield, his versatility looks set to make him a regular presence in Hansi Flick's resurgent side. Blessed with an immaculate sense of timing and an ability to drift into space unnoticed, Musiala, at just 20, will surely help to keep the German midfield ticking over for several tournaments to come.

AO TANAKA

⚽ **Being given a chance in professional football is one thing.** Seizing it with both hands is quite another. When injuries presented Tanaka with an opportunity to cement a place in Kawasaki Frontale's midfield, he displayed a maturity beyond his years, proving himself to be a robust yet measured defensive midfielder. After winning the J League Rookie of the Year Aware he was called up for Japan. Once again he pounced on the chance, helping Japan to beat shock Germany 2-1 in Qatar before scoring the winner against Spain.

DARWIN NÚÑEZ

⚽ **Uruguayan. Combustible. Tenacious. Supremely talented.** Liverpool fans have seen this all before, and if the Reds' striker can emulate his fellow countryman Luis Suárez he'll be a snip at £85 million. Uruguay will also be hoping Núñez can follow Suárez's international example. A return of three goals in 16 games isn't quite Suarez level yet, but Núñez, who admittedly endured a poor World Cup in Qatar as Uruguay crashed out in the group stages, is hardly scared of a challenge. Still only 24, he has plenty of time to make a name for himself on the international stage. Establishing a starting spot in Liverpool's first XI would be a major step in the right direction.

AURÉLIEN TCHOUAMÉNI

⚽ **When Real Madrid are willing to part with €100 million (including add-ons) in order to beat Liverpool to your signature, you're doing something right.** In the case of Tchouaméni, he's been getting a whole lot right since emerging at Bordeaux in 2018. A developing presence at the base of both Real and France's midfield, the UEFA Nations League winner has assuaged any concerns about unearthing N'Golo Kanté's successor. Admittedly he has some way to go before he can claim to be at Kanté's attack-extinguishing level, but with time on his side, one suspects that Tchouaméni (who scored against England at the 2022 World Cup) may one day retire with a trophy cabinet to rival the legend his appears destined to replace.

WORLD CUP LEGENDS

MOMENTS
3 JULY 2018
ENGLAND WIN A SHOOTOUT

The Three Lions finally exorcised the ghosts of the past to clinch victory in a tense penalty shootout with Colombia

England fans the world over emitted an audible sigh when referee Mike Geiger blew the whistle on a nervy period of extra time during which both the Three Lions and Colombia had failed to engineer a winner in their Round of 16 clash in the Spartak Stadium in Moscow. Victory had been but seconds away when Yerry Mina headed home a stoppage-time equaliser for the South Americans, and now, to make matters worse, England faced penalties.

Since tasting defeat on spot kicks against West Germany in the semi-finals at Italia '90, England had lost another five penalty shootouts; twice at subsequent World Cups and three times at the European Championships. Needless to say, hopes were not high among the English contingent watching on from the stands. They need not have worried.

Falcao put Colombia 1-0 up with the first effort of the shootout, but England skipper Harry Kane calmly pulled England level. Marcus Rashford then did likewise with England's second penalty to make it 2-2. But then disaster struck, David Ospina guessing correctly to dive to his left and tip Jordan Henderson's effort away. It all felt too familiar, another heartbreak seemingly just a few kicks away. Then, to the relief of every England fan, Colombia hit the upright.

Afforded this unexpected reprieve, England drew level again before Jordan Pickford then parried Carlos Bacca's effort away to safety, presenting Eric Dier with the chance to win a World Cup shootout for England for the first time. The Spurs man didn't disappoint, rifling the ball into the net to send England into the quarter-finals.

WORLD CUP LEGENDS

TOP 10: UPSETS

Reckon a team is a sure-fire winner? Don't bet on it: football can be a funny old game, as these shock results have proved

EAST GERMANY 1 WEST GERMANY 0, 1974

Packed with footballing superstars and with the World Cup tournament played on their own home turf, West Germany were clear favourites in Hamburg against an East Germany side made up of relatively unknown part-timers. Jürgen Sparwasser scored the only goal in the 77th minute, and the 1,500 East German fans allowed to travel went crazy.

BULGARIA 2 GERMANY 1, 1994

It was no surprise that mighty Germany - the defending champions who were representing a unified country for the first time since 1938 - would reach the quarter-finals in 1994. But nobody expected rank outsiders Bulgaria to score two goals in two minutes with just 15 minutes to go.

PERU 3 SCOTLAND 1, 1978

Scotland were Britain's only representatives at the World Cup in Argentina in 1978, and such was the hype around their participation, a stamp was even produced declaring their World Cup win. It was never released. They fell to a shock 3-1 opening defeat against Peru and were ultimately knocked out at the group stage.

SPAIN 0 NORTHERN IRELAND 1, 1982

Northern Ireland had qualified for the World Cup for the first time since 1958, and they were playing against the host nation and early favourites, Spain. But even though Mal Donaghy was sent off, leaving Northern Ireland with just ten men for the final 30 minutes, Gerry Armstrong's goal was enough to secure victory.

SENEGAL 1 FRANCE 0, 2002

Defending champions France had a real stinker of a tournament in 2002, failing to score a single goal and finding themselves bottom of Group A. Former French colony Senegal got the ball of misery rolling in the opening game - their first ever in a World Cup - as Papa Bouba Diop netted from two yards out.

TOP 10: UPSETS

NORTH KOREA 1 ITALY 0, 1966
With the Korean War still fresh in many minds, North Korea's participation in 1966 was almost scuppered by the British government's reluctance to grant the team visas. But after a bit of to-ing and fro-ing, the secretive side were allowed entry and, thanks to right-winger Pak Doo-ik, they promptly knocked one of the favourites, Italy, out of the tournament.

ARGENTINA 0 CAMEROON 1, 1990
A Cameroon side largely made up of journeymen from the French lower divisions found themselves up against champions Argentina in the first game of Italia '90. The underdogs went in hard, earning themselves two red cards but successfully neutralising Argentina's star man Diego Maradona. With François Omam-Biyik's 67th-minute strike, Cameroon bagged the game's only goal and proved the better side.

USA 1 ENGLAND 0, 1950
To highlight the gulf between these two sides, the amateur and semi-professional USA team included a postman, a funeral director and a mill-worker. England, meanwhile, had been dubbed the 'Kings of Football'. Yet when the Americans took the lead in the first half, thanks to a goal by Joe Gaetjens in the 38th minute, they held firm. Much-fancied England were humiliated.

SAUDI ARABIA 2 ARGENTINA 1, 2022
In what was statistically the biggest shock in World Cup history, minnows Saudi Arabia outfoxed and outfought Argentina in Qatar. Afforded just an 8.7 per cent chance of victory prior to the Group C opener, the Green Falcons recovered from falling behind to a Lionel Messi penalty to strike twice in the second half to stun the eventual champions and secure Saudi Arabia's fourth win in 17 games at the World Cup.

WEST GERMANY 3 HUNGARY 2, 1954
Back in 1954, Hungary were known as the Mighty Magyars and between 1950 and 1956, they had suffered just one defeat: this match. Known for their 'Total Football', they had actually smashed West Germany 8-3 just 14 days earlier in their Group Two match on 20 June 1954. But here the two sides were meeting in the final on 4 July and everybody had written the Germans off. Certainly, in the first eight minutes of the game, Hungary successfully proved their might. Led by Ferenc Puskás, who was named the 1954 tournament's best player, they were quickly 2-0 up. But then West Germany hit back in the 10th, 18th and 84th minutes and jaws dropped around the world. The game became known as the Miracle of Berne, while the Hungarian Revolution of 1956 saw a once-great team sadly ripped apart.

WORLD CUP LEGENDS

MOMENTS

18 DECEMBER 2022

KING OF THE WORLD

After years of heartache football's greatest player finally clinches the ultimate prize

Sometimes it's just not meant to be. As he trudged from the pitch and into the bowels of the Maracanã Stadium in the wake of Argentina's crushing 1-0 defeat to Germany in the 2014 World Cup final, Messi must have been shadowed by the thought that he would never get a better opportunity to win the tournament. Further frustration would follow in 2018 at the hands of eventual winners France, and by the time he was heading out to Qatar in the winter of 2022 at the age of 35, Messi was confronted with a sobering reality: this was (in all likelihood) his last chance to land the big one and, despite his shimmering career to date, avoid a retirement spent wondering what it would have felt like to stand alongside Maradona as a world champion. As things would transpire, he wouldn't have much longer to wait.

Orchestrating La Albiceleste in the manner of a conductor possessed, Messi somehow contrived to elevate his game to a new level. Rallying his teammates in the aftermath of a stunning opening defeat to Saudi Arabia, Messi inspired Argentina to a crucial 2-0 win over Mexico, his crisp low drive breaking the deadlock.

He would overcome another setback (in the form of watching Poland's Wojciech Szczęsny brilliantly saving his penalty during Argentina's 2-0 triumph over the Europeans) to help dispatch a stubborn Australia in the Round of 16.

Growing into the tournament, Messi added his fourth goal of the campaign in a tense quarter-final against the Netherlands that required penalties to separate the sides.

Croatia, finalists in 2018, lurked in the semis, but Messi paid their tournament pedigree little heed, smashing a penalty high into the net before assisting a Julián Álvarez brace in a scintillating 3-0 win.

Only holders France now stood between Lionel Scaloni's men and immortality, and on a chaotic night in Lusail, Messi was in no mood to let it slip through his hands again. Scoring twice in an enthralling encounter that ended 3-3 after extra time courtesy of Kylian Mbappé's late penalty, Argentina's captain stepped up to take his country's first spot-kick in the ensuing shootout. In a display of nonchalance that belied the enormous pressure bearing down on him, Messi casually rolled the ball beyond Hugo Lloris to set Argentina on their way.

Looking on from the halfway line as Gonzalo Montiel shaped to take the most important kick of his life, Messi collapsed to his knees as the net bulged. In a single moment of pure ecstasy and relief the burden of delivering the greatest honour in sport evaporated into the desert sky.

Finally, 16 years after scampering onto the field in Gelsenkirchen to make his World Cup debut as a wavy-haired prodigy, Messi the man had reached the stars and emulated the achievements of the late Maradona. Sometimes it's just meant to be.

KING OF THE WORLD

WORLD CUP LEGENDS

11 STARS OF THE WOMEN'S WORLD CUP 2023

A festival of football Down Under witnessed record crowds, breathtaking drama and no shortage of stunning strikes as the women's game took another crucial step forwards. Here are the players who shone brightest on the biggest stage…

LAUREN HEMP
AGE – 23 | TEAM – ENGLAND

01 After playing a peripheral role as England won Euro 2022 on home soil (although she did assist Chloe Kelly's scrambled winner in the final), many expected Man City's tireless attacker to take centre stage at the 2023 World Cup. They weren't disappointed.

Never afraid to drive her team forwards, Hemp's willingness to take opponents on was crucial for England, especially during some rather lacklustre team performances early on. Featuring in every match (starting in six) as England reached their first-ever World Cup final, Hemp developed a lethal partnership with Alessia Russo.

Constantly harrying opposition defences, Hemp was rewarded with three goals during the tournament, finding the net in a 6-1 drubbing of China before pouncing on individual errors to score against Colombia and Australia, as well as providing a beautifully weighted assist for Russo against the Matilda's to seal a 3-1 win.

Determined as ever, Hemp quickly brushed off hitting the woodwork early on in the final against Spain. Often serving as the main threat to the Spanish back line, Hemp remained on the field as Wiegman removed the rest of her attack, but sadly for the Lionesses neither Hemp nor the manager's substitutions could find a way back into the match. However, one suspects Hemp's first World Cup final may not be her last.

Hemp has scored 13 goals in 45 games for England

11 STARS OF THE WOMEN'S WORLD CUP 2023

Miyazawa's showing at the World Cup earned her a move to Manchester United

HINATA MIYAZAWA
AGE – 23 | TEAM – **JAPAN**

02 Being selected for your first World Cup is a remarkable achievement in itself, but going on to win the Golden Boot with five sumptuous goals as you help your country to the quarter-finals is something else entirely.

Echoing the feat of Homare Sawa (Golden Boot winner at the 2011 World Cup), Miyazawa was rampant in Australia and New Zealand, lashing home the opener against Zambia in Japan's first group game before ghosting in to put her side 3-0 up just after the hour mark.

After failing to find the net in a routine 2-0 defeat of Costa Rica, Miyazawa faced a slick-looking Spain in Japan's final group match. Many anticipated a close encounter, but any notions of a tight contest were obliterated by a rampant Japan, with Miyazawa running the show.

Slipped through on goal by Jun Endo, Miyazawa displayed her customary composure to slide the ball past Misa Rodriquez to snatch the lead. On the half-hour mark she set up Riko Ueki to (fortuitously) double Japan's lead before then putting the result beyond doubt with half-time looming, arcing a gorgeous strike over a dispairing Rodriquez to finish a flowing team move. A late Mina Tanaka goal capped a 4-0 evisceration of the eventual champions.

Miyazawa would score once again in the Round of 16 as Futoshi Ikeda's outfit roared past 1995 winners Norway courtesy of a 3-1 victory. Scandinavian opponents also lurked in the quarter-finals, and unfortunately for Japan, Sweden proved to be far less accomodating. Careful not to fall into Japan's counter-attacking trap, the Swedes ran out 2-1 winners to book a berth in the semis.

Defeat for the impressive Japanese no doubt stung, but they can console themselves with the fact that in Miyazawa they have a star who will no doubt plunder plenty more goals in the future and will only be 27 at the next World Cup.

HAYLEY RASO
AGE – 28 | TEAM – **AUSTRALIA**

03 To watch Hayley Raso's performances for the 2023 World Cup co-hosts you would never guess at the incredible hurdles she had to overcome not just to play the game she loves but simply to walk. In the summer of 2018 the former Man City attacker suffered a serious back injury that left doctors questioning whether she'd ever walk again, let alone kick a ball in anger. Hellbent on making a full recovery, Raso threw herself into rehabilitation and, just six months later, she was scoring against rivals New Zealand at the 2019 Cup of Nations.

Fast forward four years and she was at it again on home soil, displaying excellent control to rifle the first of two goals into the Canadian net in a 4-0 drubbing of the North Americans. Named Player of the Match, Raso continued her goalscoring exploits in a 2-0 victory against a stubborn Denmark as the Matildas marched into the quarter-finals.

The first Australian to pull on the famous white shirt of Real Madrid, Raso continues to prove what an exceptional talent she is. Elevated to unprecedented heights Down Under thanks to the 2023 World Cup, football in Australia looks set to flourish, and any budding young player can take serious inspiration from this silky forward with a mind of steel.

Raso joined Real Madrid on a free transfer in July 2023

123

○ At the time of writing Arsenal have made two bids to sign Earps

LINDA CAICEDO
AGE - 18 | TEAM - COLOMBIA

04 Competing at a World Cup was never going to daunt Colombia's young tyro. Despite her youth, she had already confronted far more terrifying situations.

After making her international debut at 14, Caicedo was given the type of news that nobody ever wants to hear: she had cancer. At 15. Surgery on her ovaries would be required followed by six months of chemotherapy. Devastated by the diagnosis and wondering if she would ever play again, Caicedo, with the support of her family, friends and coach, battled through, and she was back in training mere days after completing her treatment.

When the time came to represent Colombia at their third World Cup, Caicedo seized her chance. With less than 40 minutes of her tournament debut on the clock she dribbled at a withdrawing South Korean back line, cut inside and bent a long-range shot towards goal that proved too powerful for Yoon Younggeul to keep out, making Caicedo the second-youngest South American to find the net at a Women's World Cup.

She would do so for a second time in Colombia's next match against Germany. With the ball ricocheting to her inside the box, Caicedo had it all to do as two defenders closed in. Displaying a composure that belied her years, the Colombian skipped between them and curled a delicious strike into the top corner. Germany later drew level, but on a truly

○ Caicedo's goal against Germany was voted as the best strike of the tournament

memorable day for the Powerpuff Girls (yes, really) Manuela Vanegas steered home a 97th-minute header to snatch a famous win.

Ultimately, Colombia's journey would end in the quarter-finals at the hands of finalists England, but not before Caicedo assisted Leicy Santos' speculative opener. A growing force in the women's game, Colombia will be back, as will Caicedo.

"She wants the ball, never hides, she's from another planet, entirely unique," beamed Colombia assistant coach Angelo Marsiglia. If the world didn't know that before, it certainly does now.

MARY EARPS
AGE - 30 | TEAM - ENGLAND

05 Hailed as the greatest shot stopper currently playing in women's football, Mary Earps is at the very top of her game. But it wasn't always plaudits and accolades for the Nottingham-born Manchester United keeper.

Selected by Phil Neville as England's third-choice goalkeeper for the 2019 World Cup in France, Earps spent the tournament kicking her studs on the bench. Her situation then worsened in the November of that year when, in the wake of a 2-1 home defeat to Germany, Neville banished Earps into the international wilderness. Such was her despair that she actually considered quitting the game altogether. Then along came Sarina Wiegman.

Spotting potential in the young keeper, the Lionesses' newly appointed manager made Earps her number one. It was a decision that would pay off handsomely as England went 30 games unbeaten, a streak that included winning Euro 2022, the nation's first footballing honour since 1966.

Rightly retaining her spot for the 2023 World Cup, Earps continued to make vital saves for England as they navigated their way to the final. Among a host of stellar interventions were a match-winning save to deny Haiti's Roseline Eloissant in the group stages, a strong hand to prevent Colombia drawing level in the quarter-finals and a well-judged penalty save against Spain's Jenni Hermosa to keep England in the final.

Although she would no doubt swap it for a winner's medal, Earps was awarded the Golden Glove, having already won FIFA's Best Women's Goalkeeper 2022 trophy in February. The subject of a world-record £100,000 bid from Arsenal just days after the final (a bid Man United unsurprisingly rejected), few would bet against Earps adding further prizes to her mantlepiece – perhaps one day the greatest one of all.

11 STARS OF THE WOMEN'S WORLD CUP 2023

REGGAE GIRLZ
TEAM – JAMAICA

06 The Jamaican women's team qualified for the country's first World Cup in 2019. It was a sobering experience that heralded three straight Group C defeats to Brazil, Italy and Australia with 12 goals conceded and just a solitary strike for the debutants. In fact, so generous were Jamaica that an opposition player registered a hat-trick in every game, with Sam Kerr scoring four for Australia.

Predicating their approach on a solid back line, Lorne Donaldson's side arrived at the 2023 edition determined to give their illustrious Group F rivals a fight. They would begin by holding 2019 hosts France to a goalless draw before beating Panama (competing in their first World Cup) 1-0.

Brazil awaited Jamaica in their final group game. Most experts expected that Marta and co would recover from their 2-1 loss to France and sweep their plucky Caribbean opponents aside, but the Reggae Girlz refused to dance to anyone's tune except their own. Standing firm in the face of relentless attacks, Jamaica managed to frustrate Brazil and claim a hugely impressive point in a 0-0 draw, a result that condemned Pia Sundhage's side to elimination.

Yet another resolute performance in the Round of 16 restricted Colombia to few opportunities, but eventually the South Americans found a way past Rebecca Spencer courtesy of Catalina Usme's goal.

Even though the party was over, Jamaica headed home knowing they'd done their people proud.

Skipper Khadija Shaw (back row, far right) has scored 56 goals in just 36 games for Jamaica

AITANA BONMATÍ
AGE – 25 | TEAM – SPAIN

07 Small. Extremely skillful. Came through La Masia to win the game's biggest prizes for Barcelona and Spain. Sound familiar? However, we're not talking about Xavi or Iniesta. This description in fact applies to a technically superb young woman who once based her game on the legendary duo.

Blessed with impeccable timing and an ability to slow the game down or speed it up as required, Bonmatí seemed to be everywhere at once for Spain at the World Cup, completing 44 line-breaking passes and achieving a tournament-leading 86 per cent pass-completion rate in the opposition's half.

After deftly evading a defender to sweep home against Costa Rica in Spain's opening 3-0 triumph, Bonmatí bossed proceedings against Switzerland in the Round of 16. A gorgeous turn inside the penalty area opened up the space for her to put Spain ahead, and she then fizzed in a cross for Alba Redondo to nod in Spain's second.

The diminutive maestro continued to torment the stricken Swiss, sitting Gaelle Thalmann down and then dinking the ball over a host of onrushing defenders to make it 3-1. As the clock reached 70 minutes an expertly weighted first-time through ball sent Jenni Hermosa in on goal to complete a 5-1 rout.

Continuing to serve as her side's engine, Bonmatí excelled against the Netherlands, Sweden and England, touching the ball 74 times in the final as Jorge Vilda's team suffocated Wiegman's side on their way to winning Spain's first trophy. When it came to handing out the Golden Ball award for the tournament's best player there wasn't really a decision to make, and it would be a major surprise if the Ballon d'Or judges don't come to the same conclusion in October.

Seen here holding the Golden Ball aloft, Bonmatí won UEFA's Women's Player of the Year Award on 31 August

WORLD CUP LEGENDS

SALMA PARALLUELO
AGE – 19 | TEAM – **SPAIN**

08 The last thing any weary defender wants to see as they attempt to shepherd their back line through the latter stages of a knockout game is a winger blessed with rapid pace and elastic control stepping onto the pitch. Now imagine said winger is also a medal-winning 400-metre hurdle-jumping athlete and you can start to picture just how devastating a player Salma Paralluelo is.

After failing to make much of an impact in each of Spain's three group games, Barcelona's dreadlocked speed demon lost her starting place for the Round of 16 destruction of Switzerland. She was then benched again in the quarter-final against the Dutch. If coach Jorge Vilda was hoping to provoke Paralluelo into proving a point, then his tactic of holding her back only to unleash her at the opportune moment worked perfectly.

Locked at 1-1 in extra time, Spain and the Netherlands seemed to be probing their way through a cagey additional 30 minutes before the lottery of a penalty shootout. Fortunately for the Iberians, Paralluelo, introduced on 71 minutes, had other ideas. Sent into space by a neat ball from Hermoso, Paralluelo bolted into space and honed in on goal. A nifty step-over created just enough room to slam the ball past Daphne van Domselaar and into the bottom corner to send the Spanish bench into raptures and La Roja into the semi-finals.

Restricted to the bench again in the semi-final against Sweden despite her earlier heroics, Paralluelo once more proved the difference in a nail-biting contest, rifling home Spain's first shot on target in a match they would ultimately win 2-1. She nearly scored again in the final against England but her instinctive snap shot kissed the post.

A world champion before her 20th birthday, Paralluelo surely won't find herself on the bench too many times in the future. Her efforts throughout Spain's triumphant campaign rightly warranted the prize for the tournament's Best Young Player, and the odds will be pretty short on her winning the Golden Ball in 2027.

Paralluelo won two medals at the 2019 European Youth Summer Olympic Festival

Sweden's number one is part of a strong roster of keepers at Chelsea

ZEĆIRA MUŠOVIĆ
AGE – 27 | TEAM – **SWEDEN**

09 Encouraged to try football by her older brother, Mušović (who moved from Bosnia to Sweden as a child) fell in love with the beautiful game and began to show such promise that by the age of nine she was admitted into the academy of her local side Stattena IF. Yet few could have guessed how far the precocious young stopper's talent would take her.

Focused on reaching the summit of her profession, Mušović enjoyed a successful club career as she climbed through the ranks at FC Rosengård in the city of Malmö. However, her international career was far from smooth sailing, and Mušović struggled for minutes until an injury to Hedvig Lindahl finally provided her with the chance to stake her claim as Sweden's number one at the World Cup.

After starting Sweden's first two group matches (a 2-1 triumph over South Africa and a 5-0 battering of Italy), Mušović was rested for the Scandinavians' 2-0 win against Argentina. Their reward for topping the group was a Round-of-16 clash with holders USA, but if the prospect daunted Mušović she certainly didn't show it.

The Americans rediscovered the cutting edge they had sorely lacked in the first round and peppered Mušović's goal throughout normal and extra time, but in the Chelsea keeper they met an unrelenting adversary. Making a record 11 saves (by a goalkeeper to keep a clean sheet in a Women's World Cup game), some of them truly jaw-dropping, Mušović denied the USA at every turn and was the only reason that the Swedes survived to reach a penalty shootout, one they would eventually win 5-4.

Rightly hailed for her exceptional showing, Mušović would go on to help her country reach the semi-finals, where Spain proved too strong. A third-place playoff presented Mušović with one last opportunity to claim another shutout, and once again she didn't disappoint, frustrating Australia in a 2-0 win that secured Sweden a second successive bronze medal. Many argued afterwards that Mušović, and not Mary Earps, should have been flying home with the Golden Glove in her luggage.

AMANDA ILESTEDT
AGE – 30 | TEAM – **SWEDEN**

11 It's often argued that the contributions of centre backs are all too readily overlooked, but when a defender dominates both boxes and scores four goals en route to a World Cup third-place finish they become a little harder to miss, and no one could possibly dismiss Amanda Ilestedt's 2023 bronze-winning campaign.

Robust, calm and dominant in the air, Arsenal's new commander ran a tight defence that kept clean sheets against Italy, Argentina, the USA and Australia. Job done from a defensive perspective, but she didn't stop there.

Demonstrating her excellent sense of timing, Ilstedt scored a 90th-minute winner against South Africa and then headed not one but two corners into the net against Italy. After shutting the holders out in the Round of 16, she put Sweden 1-0 up against Japan in the quarter-finals. Leading from the back throughout, this vocal defender was unlucky to be on the losing side in the semis and fully deserved the Bronze Ball Award.

○ Ilstedt played for Bayern Munich and PSG prior to her move to London

OLGA CARMONA
AGE – 23 | TEAM – **SPAIN**

10 Real Madrid's marauding full-back doesn't score many, but when you drive in the winner in a World Cup semi-final and then follow that up with the only goal in the final to secure your nation's first Women's World Cup, you don't need to.

After starting all three group games, Carmona was forced to battle her way back into contention for the semi-final versus Sweden. Not only did she regain her place but she proceeded to settle the contest with a dipping strike from range as the clock approached 90 minutes.

Unaware that her father had sadly passed away the day prior to the final, Carmona went one better against England, arrowing Mariona Caldentey's pass beyond Mary Earps to cap a flowing counter-attack and snatch glory.

Speaking on the day after the final, she paid a beautiful tribute to her late father.

"I have no words to thank [you for] all your love. Yesterday was the best and worst day of my life. I know that you would like to see me enjoy this historic moment, that is why I will be with my colleagues, so that from wherever you are you know that this star is also yours, dad."

○ Off the field Carmona is studying for a degree in Physical Activity and Sports Sciences

WORLD CUP LEGENDS

MOMENTS

16 AUGUST 2023

HALTING MATILDA

England's Lionesses finally bare their fangs in a ruthless mauling of the hosts

England doesn't exactly boast a history of winning semi-finals, and it certainly doesn't have a track record of outplaying a well-backed host nation en route to a 3-1 victory and a place in a World Cup final for the first time. But then there's never been a team like Sarina Wiegman's Lionesses before.

Tipped to go far Down Under, England arrived in Australia as reigning European champions who had developed a habit of finding a way past even the most stubborn opponents. It was a trait they would rely on in the weeks ahead as they laboured to narrow wins over Haiti and Denmark. While China were thrashed 6-1, England regressed to their (uncharacteristically) lethargic ways against Nigeria and Colombia as they navigated a rocky path to a semi-final clash against co-hosts Australia.

Several well-informed pundits backed England to edge a close encounter, and yet, despite the score being level at 1-1 on 70 minutes thanks to Sam Kerr's outrageous long-range strike, in truth Wiegman's team dominated proceedings. Controlling 59 per cent of possession and executing 480 passes to 331 (with an accuracy of 83 per cent against Australia's 74 per cent), England largely smothered the Matildas.

Constantly harrying the hosts, England pounced with 20 minutes left to restore their lead through Lauren Hemp's opportunistic finish. Not satisfied to simply see the game out, the Lionesses went for the kill, and on 86 minutes their tenacity was rewarded.

Played into space by a deftly disguised pass from Hemp, Alessia Russo surged into the box and swept a neat angled shot beyond Mackenzie Arnold to shatter Aussie dreams and send England into the final.

HALTING MATILDA

WORLD CUP LEGENDS

Future PLC Quay House, The Ambury, Bath, BA1 1UA

Bookazine Editorial
Editors **Dan Peel & Charles Ginger**
Designers **Perry Wardell-Wicks & Thomas Parrett**
Head of Art & Design **Greg Whitaker**
Editorial Director **Jon White**
Managing Director **Grainne McKenna**

Cover images
Getty Images, Alamy

Photography
All copyrights and trademarks are recognised and respected

Advertising
Media packs are available on request
Commercial Director **Clare Dove**

International
Head of Print Licensing **Rachel Shaw**
licensing@futurenet.com
www.futurecontenthub.com

Circulation
Head of Newstrade **Tim Mathers**

Production
Head of Production **Mark Constance**
Production Project Manager **Matthew Eglinton**
Advertising Production Manager **Joanne Crosby**
Digital Editions Controller **Jason Hudson**
Production Managers **Keely Miller, Nola Cokely, Vivienne Calvert, Fran Twentyman**

Printed in the UK

Distributed by Marketforce, 5 Churchill Place, Canary Wharf, London, E14 5HU
www.marketforce.co.uk – For enquiries, please email:
mfcommunications@futurenet.com

This book is 100% unofficial and unaffiliated with FIFA or the FIFA World Cup

World Cup Legends Sixth Edition (SBZ5612)
© 2023 Future Publishing Limited

We are committed to only using magazine paper which is derived from responsibly managed, certified forestry and chlorine-free manufacture. The paper in this bookazine was sourced and produced from sustainable managed forests, conforming to strict environmental and socioeconomic standards.

All contents © 2023 Future Publishing Limited or published under licence. All rights reserved. No part of this magazine may be used, stored, transmitted or reproduced in any way without the prior written permission of the publisher. Future Publishing Limited (company number 2008885) is registered in England and Wales. Registered office: Quay House, The Ambury, Bath BA1 1UA. All information contained in this publication is for information only and is, as far as we are aware, correct at the time of going to press. Future cannot accept any responsibility for errors or inaccuracies in such information. You are advised to contact manufacturers and retailers directly with regard to the price of products/services referred to in this publication. Apps and websites mentioned in this publication are not under our control. We are not responsible for their contents or any other changes or updates to them. This magazine is fully independent and not affiliated in any way with the companies mentioned herein.

FUTURE Connectors. Creators. Experience Makers.

Future plc is a public company quoted on the London Stock Exchange (symbol: FUTR)
www.futureplc.com

Chief Executive Officer **Jon Steinberg**
Non-Executive Chairman **Richard Huntingford**
Chief Financial and Strategy Officer **Penny Ladkin-Brand**

Tel +44 (0)1225 442 244